YOUR DOOR TO ARABIA

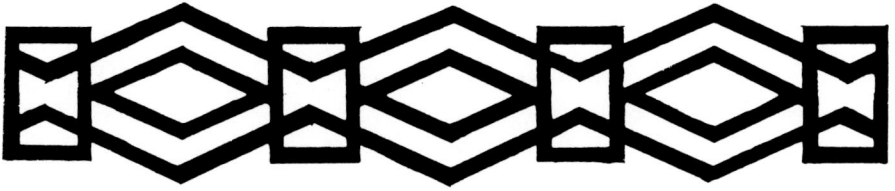

YOUR DOOR TO
ARABIA

Written and Illustrated by

Jeri Elliott

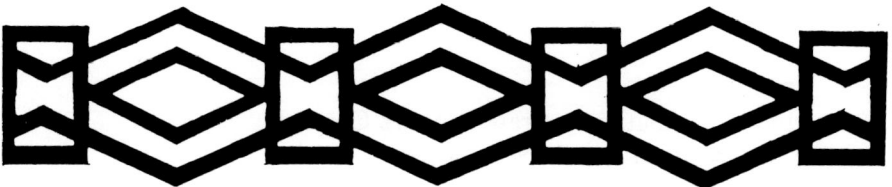

Published by the Author
C/- P.O. Box 99, Invercargill, New Zealand

ISBN 0 473 01546 3 *Second Revised Edition 1992*

First Edition 1986 (Kingdom of Saudi Arabia Ministry of Information, Registration No. 1863)

U.S. Library of Congress Catalog Number 1-91-614

Printed and distributed by Craig Printing Co. Ltd, 67 Tay Street, Invercargill, New Zealand.
1992 — 71826

DEDICATION

To Nikki and Terry, my best friends.

TABLE OF CONTENTS

Mohammed the Prophet, Zam Zam, 1001 Arabia Nights, Lawrence of Arabia, Frankincense and Myrrh, Perfumes of Arabia, A Domain of Kings, Oil! Oil!

Islam, Sunnites and Shi'aites, Impurity, The Holy Quran, Islamic Law, Prayer, The Five Pillars of Faith, The Holy Kaaba, Mosques, Prayer Beads, Hajj, Ramadan

Makka, Medina, Riyadh, Jeddah, Al Khobar, Abha, Dhahran, Hofuf, Qatif, Dammam, Jubail, Taif, Yanbu, Regions of Arabia

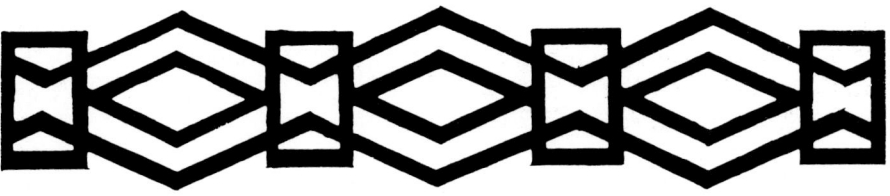

AUTHOR'S NOTE

Twelve years of living and working in the Middle East alongside the Arabic people offered the groundwork for this book. Indirect sources came from the Arabs themselves, my friends who were willing to share with me an understanding of their traditional habits of living just as their fathers had lived and their fathers' fathers. Although I had the opportunity to visit many countries in the Middle East, the two that I lived in during those twelve years were Bahrain and Saudi Arabia. Despite both countries being Islamic, and virtually on each other's doorstep, they are noticeably contrasting regions, in that within Bahrain the traditional ways and the modern have managed to live side by side harmoniously, whereas in Saudi the ways of old and contemporary life styles are forever opposing each other, the 'new ways' being illegal in many cases. For example, in Bahrain women are permitted to drive and work alongside the men, however in Saudi Arabia, women are limited to work only in hospitals or schools, and driving is strictly forbidden.

Extracts included in this book from the Quran, and other Arabic translations were interpreted for me by a close Arab friend from Makka, the holiest of cities in Saudi Arabia. This friend would rather remain anonymous due to the strict Islamic ruling of his country and the fact that just as theologians often argue over Biblical interpretations, the same holds true with the Quran.

I wish to extend special thanks to Susie Al Gahtani who opened a new world of research for me within Arabia, to all the persons who gave their help and enthusiasm, and to those who offered insight into a culture that most people will never see nor understand. A very special thank you to Penny Musacchia for the 'apple.' Without their generous support and willing assistance the groundwork and preparation of this book could never have been possible.

JERI A. ELLIOTT

INTRODUCTION

YOUR DOOR TO ARABIA, written amidst the pervading calls to prayer, presents a comprehensive glimpse at the Arabic culture, a culture fully influenced by the Islamic religion. The information within offers answers to questions, not finger pointing accusations that history often delivers, but instead gives you a collective look at the Arabs' traditional way of life, helping you to better comprehend a region caught up in the middle of centuries' old struggles. Despite the mystery and obscurity of the Arab world to those who have never visited its doorstep, let alone its interior, we are all aware that the events of the Middle East affect us, affect the entire world, controlling the economy with their ever flowing oil.

Tremendous changes occurred over night in this cradle of civilization when the oil dollars began to flow, lifting ancient Arabia up from the eighth century and virtually dropping it into the modern ways of the twentieth century. Contrasts between the modern and traditional ways of life can be seen everywhere, even with the desert Bedouin. Examples of these opposing worlds are the mud homes standing alongside multi-story office buildings and the indispensable four-wheel-drive jeep parked outside a Bedouin tent where the camel once had supremacy. The influence of the Western world and the new found wealth has not kept the Arab people from clinging to their past, from their everyday customs, most of which stem from Allah their God and Mohammed the prophet who spread the word of Allah, the word of Islam.

An age old way of life lives on in Arabia despite the invasion of western culture, dumped on them only because of the black oil beneath their sands. If not for the oil, life in the desert peninsula of Saudi Arabia would have remained cloaked in the 8th century, the West finding little need for their sand and their export of dates. Although Islam is universal throughout all Arab countries, the tales told in this book stem from the region known today as the Kingdom of Saudi Arabia, a country that clings by a thread to the traditional customs of their forefathers, a land that fights desperately to be true to Islam, to Allah, and Mohammed the Prophet.

LASTING
TRADITIONS

THE ARABIAN BEDOUIN

The bedouin are nomadic herdsmen of the Syrian, Arabian and Sahara deserts. Comprised of a rigid order of tribal groups they live today much like their grandfathers did, having roamed the desert for centuries — just subsisting — tending their camels and herds of goats and sheep while enduring the harsh summer heat and the biting winds that blow across the sands. During the cooler rainy season the bedouins usually roam into the desert in small groups tending their herds as the animals graze on the new desert growth. In the hot dry season they gather together in large groups around water sources near towns and markets.

Living in tents; woven from goat hair their possessions are meager, rugs and cushions for furniture and cookware made by local craftsmen. Colorful tent walls divide the men's section from the general living quarters where the women do the cooking and mind small children.

Bedouin hospitality is like no other. Any passerby is welcomed first by a rug spread on the ground and a glass of hot tea, then with the traditional ceremony of preparing and serving coffee. If the visitor intends to stay overnight a bedouin host will offer lodging and a meal that might include a freshly slaughtered young sheep or goat cooked and served with rice. This hospitality dictates that a stranger will not be asked his business or his destination.

12

Many bedouins have abandoned their nomadic life style and settled in the oases and cities with new occupations. For those who remain in this ancient life style everyday living has become much easier in the desert as these nomads share in the oil wealth. The Saudi government shares the oil dollars with all the Kingdom's people. This money has helped pay for expanded agriculture ventures within the vast sands by providing new water sources and has helped many of the wandering tribesmen to own four-wheel drive vehicles reducing desert travels. The pickup has become almost as much a part of the bedouin's life as the camel once was. Even after the oil dollars and Western influence the bedouin are still able to maintain their traditional ways of life.

DID YOU KNOW THAT . . .
'Arab' means the desert or its inhabitants and in the Quran the word 'Arab' is used to describe the bedouin.

WHAT'S IN A NAME

The giving of Arab names holds great significance and usually follows certain rules. For example, a child's name indicates who his or her father is and his father's father and his father's father's father. Confused? You may be but to the Arab a person's name tells you his family tree. This helps keep track of inheritance and lets one know his relatives. The parents choose the child's first name while the next names in sequence are the first names of the father, the grandfather, and the great grandfather. Usually just four are given, but in actual fact the name could continue on down the line of fathers' names. This even holds true for girls, their second, third and fourth names being the name of their father and so on — not their mother. Popular names include famous people in Islamic history like the Prophet Mohammed or his relatives like Asiya and Khadijah, his wives, or Fatima, the Prophet's daughter or Marian, the mother of Jesus.

When an Arab woman marries she does not take her husband's name as compared to most western cultures. Her ties to her family through her name remains important, she does not lose her identity.

Many Arabic names have meanings. Here are a few examples:

MALE		FEMALE	
Hassan	— good	Yasmeen	— jasmine
Hussain	— beautiful	Zahrah	— flower
Jamal	— beautiful	Joharah	— jewel
Muhsin	— charitable	Nora	— lights
Saied	— happy	Huda	— guidance
Ali	— high	Leila	— an ancient drink
Ahmen	— most highly praised	Ibtisam	— smile
Mohammed	— praised or blessed	Basmah	— smile

The often used 'Abdul' is not actually a name but means 'slave of' or 'worshipper of.' Any name that begins Abdul with one of God's 99 names indicates 'slave of God,' such as Abdullah, Abdulaziz, or Abdulrahman. Since children are given the names of their fathers they are often called as such, for example King Abdul Aziz Ibn Saud was called Son of Saud after his father whose name was Saud, 'ibn' means "son of," The King's first name was Abdul Aziz. Another form of naming is the use of 'abu' meaning father. In Arabia fathers are traditionally referred to by the name of their eldest son, for example if the son's name is Ali, the father would be called Abu Ali.

DID YOU KNOW THAT . . .
Mohammed (or the varied spelling of Muhammed) is the most commonly given name in the world.

MAJLIS

This term, majlis, a bedouin tradition, is derived from the name of the main living area in an Arab dwelling where guests are received. A majlis is a daily meeting presided over by regional rulers. Anyone may come to the majlis — from any walk of life. At this gathering, petitions are presented to the ruler, one by one, covering all sorts of matters such as family problems, money matters, new businesses, land disputes, or even requests for new sheep. Often the majlis is scheduled for the same day every week, and the rulers listen to their people's greetings and grievances no matter where they may be, even in a desert tent. This age-old custom offers the common person access straight to the top, even to the King of Saudi Arabia.

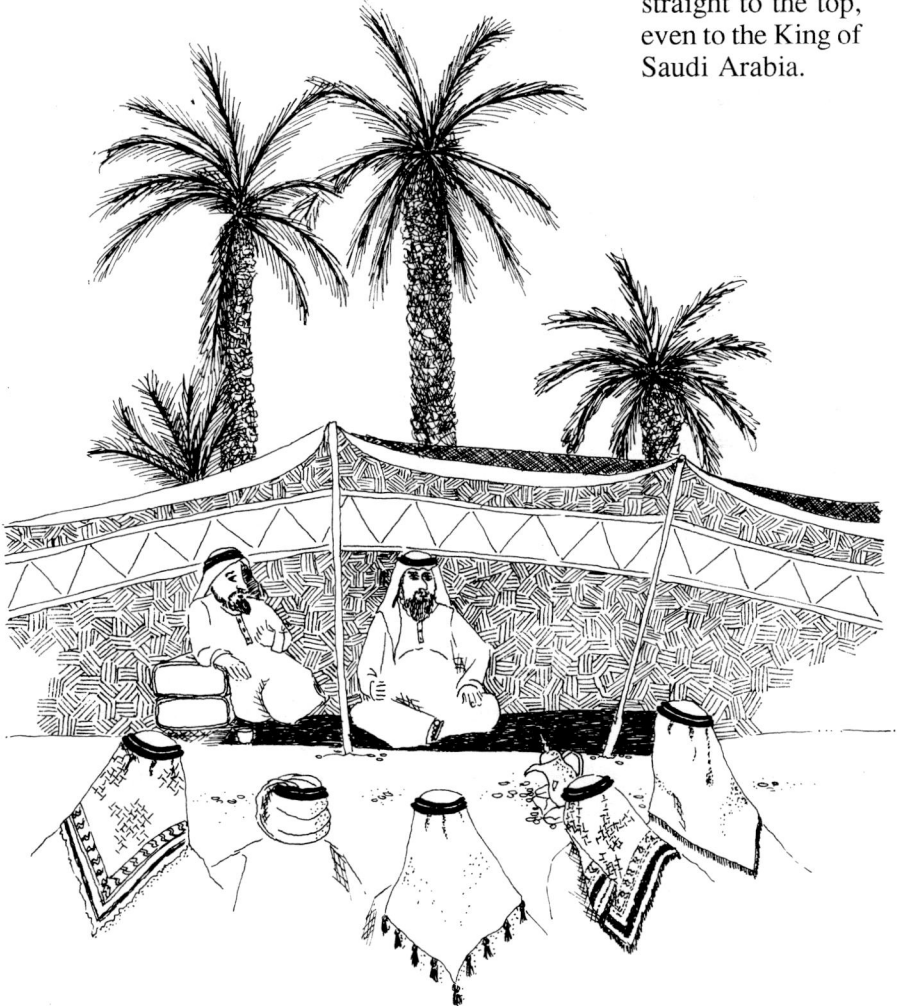

ARAB DRESS

Arab men of all backgrounds wear the traditional dress which expresses equality and the suitability to the hot desert sun, for it is often of white light-weight material. Arab men and boys wear a floor-length shirt-like dress called a 'thobe.' Thobes worn during the hot summer are usually made of white cotton, but during cold winter days heavy wool thobes of darker colors are worn. Underneath the thobe men wear shorts or long white pants. During the cooler season or at special affairs a long outer cloak called a 'bisht' or 'mishlah' is worn over the thobe made of white, brown or black material with a gold-like trimming. In the Quran; it is written that a man must cover up from his "belly to his feet." Leather sandals, like the one drawn here, are also worn by Arab men, even during the winter.

The Arab headdress consists of three parts — the 'ghutrah,' a large square of cloth; the 'tagia,' a small white skull cap that keeps the ghutrah from slipping; and the 'igal,' a doubled black cord that holds the ghutrah in place. The igal is part of the Arab's dress that belongs to the new generation, many older men are commonly seen without an igal. It is said

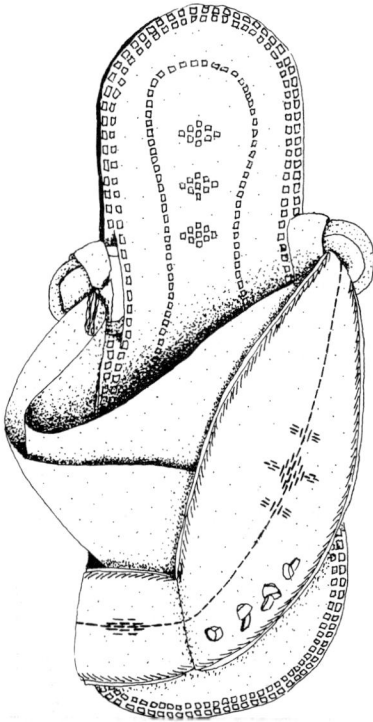

that the first three kings of Arabia wore elaborate igals, like royal crowns, threaded with real gold. The cloth of the ghutrah is often white cotton or silk folded diagonally and centered on the head like a lady's scarf, with one or more rounded points evenly shaped in the center over the forehead. The ends are tossed away from the face and shoulders, overlapping on the top of the head. Saudis are traditionally seen wearing red and white ghutrahs. Bahrainis mainly wear the solid white ghutrahs. A lesson could be learned from the Arab whose head is always covered in respect to the harsh rays of the sun.

DID YOU KNOW THAT . . .

The black cord, the igal, worn now to hold a man's headdress in place was once merely a rope used to hobble a camel's legs. While travelling the cord was doubled on the bedouin's head and during the night was placed on the camel's front legs to keep him from wandering.

16

THE ABAYAH

Unlike the appropriate white cotton desert dress of the men, the women of Arabia must wear a black capacious cloak called an 'abayah' nowadays made of silk or synthetic materials. Before the oil money brought great wealth to Saudi Arabia a woman's abayah was similar to the 'bisht' or 'mishlah,' the coarse outer cloak worn by men. Now the women can afford silk abayahs. The abayah is a large rectangle of black material doubled over in the middle, the sides stitched, and an opening on one half going from the fold at the center to the hem, and is often laced along the edges. Some abayahs have openings for the hands at the edges of the fold, creating a floor length style. The abayah is designed to completely cover the Muslim women from head to toe, however when the abayahs that do not have hand openings are worn without the arms tucked inside, the hem is lifted and draped over the arms thus creating a thigh-high style. The abayah rests on the head at the fold where the opening begins.

Along with the long black cloak women wear full face veils, placed on their head before the abayah, adding to their rightful anonymity. The veil is worn in public and even at home in the presence of male guests who are not close relatives. Other face coverings are the 'burqa,' a lightweight veil tied upon the head with openings at the eye, or the leather mask, with its eye openings, that is said to be extremely uncomfortable.

The bedouin women of the desert often do not wear veils nor abayahs, except when they are in settled areas, while still other tribal women wear a burqa that is never removed, even in the company of only women. It is said that she will remove it only when her husband requests her to do so. A variety of cloak-like coverings and veils are worn throughout Middle Eastern countries. During a trip to Iran (where the people are called Persians, not Arabs, but are still Muslims) many of the women wore abayahs of light weight material, black in color but with a printed

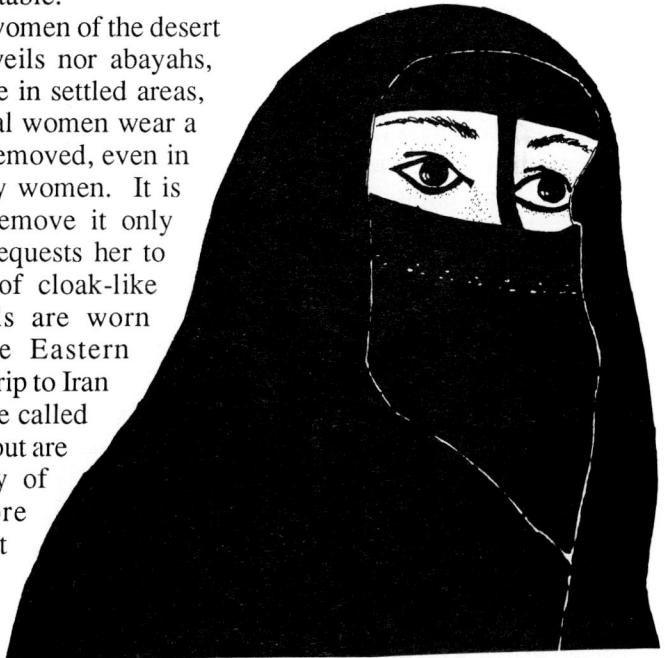

pattern, for example tiny white flowers on a black background. There is no consistency to women's coverings in the Middle East, just a tradition that dates back in history within each region.

The origin of the women's abayah in Saudi Arabia is thought to be through Turkish influence as it is said that some of the Prophet Mohammed's wives, who were from Turkey, donned dark concealing cloaks. As the Prophet spread the word of Islam he gained veneration from his followers who practiced his revealed teachings. If Mohammed's wives wore cloaks, then his followers felt their wives should cover up as well, establishing a tradition in respect to Mohammed.

There are varying interpretations of the Quran regarding the abayah and veil. Allah revealed to Mohammed that women must cover themselves from their wrists to their ankles in loose fitting clothes, and all of their hair must be covered. It is also written that a woman of exceptional beauty or those with much makeup should cover their faces.

A women's fashion, however, does not stop with the abayah although that is all you are likely to see. Beneath the black cloak Arab women enjoy fashionable dressing and take great pride in their appearance. They enjoy bright colors, lavish material and eloborate dress designs. A traditional item that is typical of the Eastern province is the delicately embroidered overgarment made of a lightweight mesh material. It is calf-length with opened sides and head opening with gold embroidery designs around the neck and front, (sometimes real gold thread is used, obviously increasing the cost). Each province of Saudi, let alone other regions in the Middle East, has their own unique traditional dress styles, enabling you to recognize where a woman comes from by her dress. Amongst the educated and wealthy women living in the cities of Arabia, the latest Paris fashions are often found underneath the black cloak and veil, as well as designs created from photographs in fashion magazines by local tailors.

❁❁❁❁❁❁ ❁❁ ❁❁❁❁❁❁❁❁❁❁❁❁❁❁❁❁❁❁❁❁❁❁❁❁

WOMEN IN ARAB CULTURE

Although the traditional role of women in Saudi Arabia has changed along with modernization most customs have remained as they were centuries ago. Saudi women still live in privacy and wear the veil outside the home. They are not seen unveiled even inside their home by men outside the immediate family. In their secluded life they often view the outside world through the closely carved wooden screened balconies that allow them the vantage point of seeing without being seen, much as their veil and black cloak provide them while in public. At their homes visitors are segregated with the women gathering in separate rooms from the men.

Segregation begins early, with the young boys and girls beginning their education in separate schools. The complicated rules of segregation protect women from gossip if they do not associate with males outside their family circle.

Women do not drive at all in Saudi, not even bicycles, nor do they work in stores or offices. They are, however employed as doctors and teachers in the many hospitals and schools throughout the Kingdom. There are even women's banks, for women, and where only women may be employed. Don't be misled, however, for the women of Arabia are not entrapped in their life styles and they will be the first to tell you so, nor are they considered inferior because of this way of life, instead they are highly respected and pampered.

HENNA

Henna, a dye used in the Middle East and Orient, comes in red and black powder, with red henna being the most commonly used. The source of the powder is from a tropical shrub, the shoots and leaves are used to make this dye. Arab women highlight their hair with henna and paint the palms of their hands and the soles of their feet to enhance their beauty just as western women might dye their hair or paint

their fingernails.

The night before a wedding is often called 'halat al-henna' (night of henna), as the bride and other women of the household spend the evening together having their hands and feet painted with henna in beautiful designs and perhaps even their hair will be enhanced. All of this is done in preparation for the wedding. Their hands are held aloft, unoccupied, and their feet are propped on pillows for hours waiting for the drying henna paste to stain their skin. After a design of henna paste dries lemon juice is squeezed over the palm and it is left for 2 or 3 hours before being washed off with water. The henna painters, servants or younger girls of the household, wait on the women as the henna-filled hands cannot even hold a glass of sugary tea.

Most older women simply hold a pack of henna in their hands giving their palms an all-over red or black look. Women who pack the henna in a tight fist wrap their hands in towels and sleep with it overnight. Others have designs painted with a toothpick or a needle, creating a fine intricate work of patterns from their finger tips to the bottom of their palm. In the souq you can buy patterns for the hands for henna designs. The longer the henna paste remains before washing off the longer the staining color will last. How long the color lasts also depends on how much housework the woman does which would wear the color off even quicker.

Even men use henna to color their hair or beards and it is said by the elderly to cure headaches. Here is a henna recipe that can be used on the hair or to paint your hands and feet.

Prepare one cup of strong hot tea (i.e., one cup of hot water and six tea bags). Place two dried black limes in the tea (black limes are found through the Middle East, in the Western world these could be omitted if unable to locate). While the tea is still hot mix with enough henna powder to make a thick paste. Allow to cool then apply to the hair like shampoo, working it into the roots for an all-over coloring, or apply it randomly for a highlighting effect. Blondes beware because you will get more than a highlight, your hair will go very red. Leave the henna on for 3 or 4 hours or overnight with your hair wrapped in a towel. Wash with warm water — no shampoo this first day — followed by a cool water rinse. The paste from the same recipe is used to paint designs on the palms of the hands or color the soles of your feet. I recommend doing one hand a day if you have no one to wait on you hand and foot!

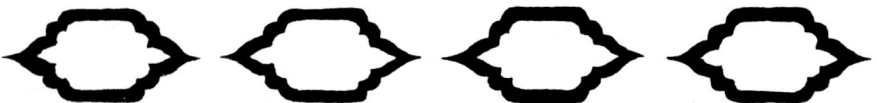

ARAB MARRIAGES

All over the world weddings are important social events when friends and relatives come to visit, some often travelling from long distances, to participate in the wedding activities. Throughout the varying regions of Arabia there are an assortment of wedding customs but there is always sure to be plenty of eating and dancing at the parties. Segregation between men and women is evident with the men having their own separate party with perhaps Arab music and a capacious meal of lamb, rice, dates, flat pita bread, side dishes and coffee.

The women's party consists of the music of drums, singing and dancing. Coffee, tea, and dates are served in abundance before the traditional Arab meal of lamb and rice. After the meal, served late in the evening, the bride often arrives to greet her guests. At some wedding parties the groom, the only man in sight, will appear with his bride and all the women who are not related will cover up. Sitting upon their elaborately adorned chairs of honor, the bride and groom are greeted and congratulated by the women. The music continues and many women will dance before the newlyweds.

The bride's dress need not be a specific color. Style and color, including white, differ from one province to another. The groom dons the traditional Arab dress of the white thobe and headdress. Many cities and villages have designated buildings where wedding parties are held, but the typical flat roof tops of the bride or groom's family home or hotel banquet halls are also popular modern day locations for wedding parties.

If men and women are continually segregated you may wonder how they meet in the first place. Most marriages are arranged by the families, even in this day and age, although the progress of the region has somewhat altered this age old custom. Marriages between cousins occur, but many marry outside their family or tribe. A son's mother may look for a wife for him, as she will have the access to meeting young girls. Upon finding a suitable prospect arrangements

21

for marriage begin between the two families. The girl is asked if she would like to marry the boy, if she agrees engagement papers are signed.

In some families today the boy and girl are allowed to see each other before the wedding day in the company of relatives while others do not tolerate these meetings, and instead photos are exchanged. The wedding day may take place anytime after engagement papers are signed by all the concerned persons. Some couples may wait 3 or 4 years, with the date usually set by the bride and groom. Marriage styles and procedures vary from one province to the next. There may be a small ceremony before a Judge with only the fathers of the two families attending with the bride's father marrying them through the Judge when formal papers are signed. In some ceremonies, the bride and groom attend. The night of the wedding parties is the night that the bride returns home with her husband.

In Islam, according to the Holy Quran, a man can legally marry up to four wives, even today, as long as he provides equally for all of them — this equality means fairly, justly, morally and economically. The condition of multi-marriages is impossible for most men to uphold therefore most take only one wife.

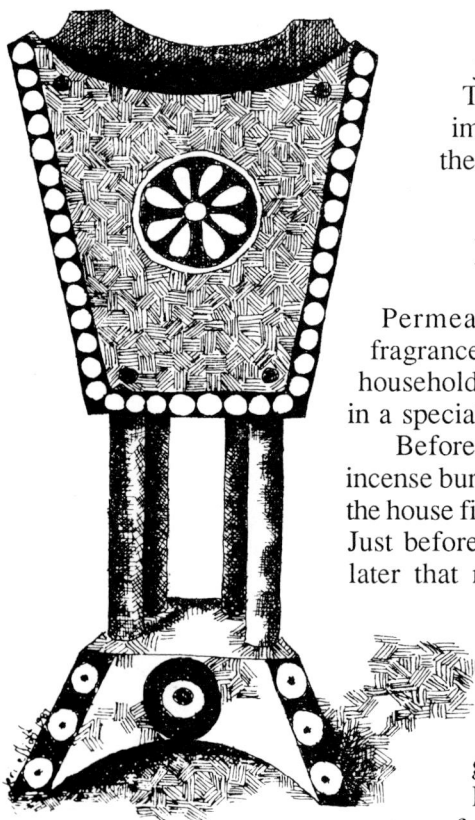

INCENSE BURNER

Permeating the atmosphere with the fragrance of incense is common to all Saudi households. Incense is burned on hot coals in a special burner called a 'mebkhara.'

Before guests arrive at a Saudi home an incense burner is prepared and carried through the house filling it with a welcoming fragrance. Just before it is time for the guests to leave later that night the host will bring out the burning incense and allow each guest to take a waft of smoke, signaling that it is time to go. Incense burners are a common sight at weddings and most social gatherings.

Burning incense is used as a perfume for the hair, body and clothes.

The aroma of the fanned smoke can last up to two or three days in the hair.

Sandalwood, or 'ouda,' is the most commonly used incense. Sandalwood is very expensive, a small handful of the hard chunks can cost a thousand riyals (equivalent NZ$500)! Incense burners are made of unbaked clay, stone or brass, and are often decorated with small mirrors. As tradition has made way for modernization, you can even buy imported electrical aluminium censors!

SHEESHAH

The 'sheeshah' or 'hubble-bubble,' is a water pipe used for smoking tobacco leaves. Tobacco leaves are laid upon hot coals in the upper dish. The smoker inhales through a long hose attached to the lower jar that holds water. The smoke is cooled as it filters through the water before being inhaled. Often dried fruit is also smoked instead of the tobacco leaves. Throughout the Middle East a common sight is the coffee house with long benches where the men sit, enjoying the 'sheeshah' while they sip the sugary tea or the aromatic cardamom spiced coffee.

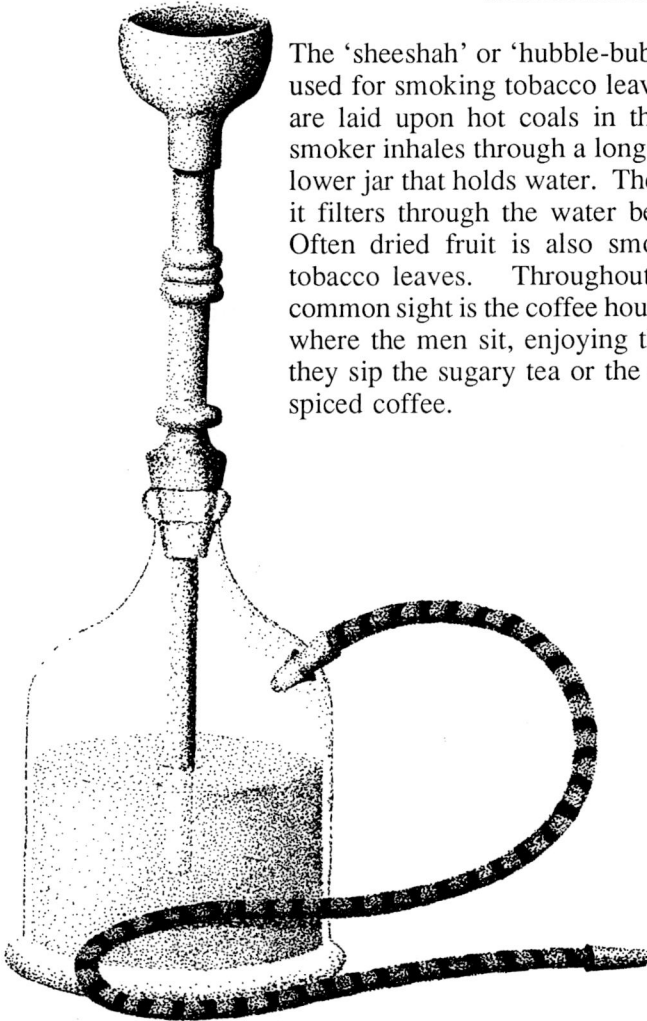

ARAB COFFEE

2 tablespoons ground coffee
4 cups cold water
2 teaspoons of ground cardamom
pinch of saffron

In a coffee pot add ground coffee to cold water. Bring pot to boil and boil for five minutes. Remove from heat. In a serving pot add ground cardamom, sugar to taste, and saffron to the strained coffee. ENJOY!

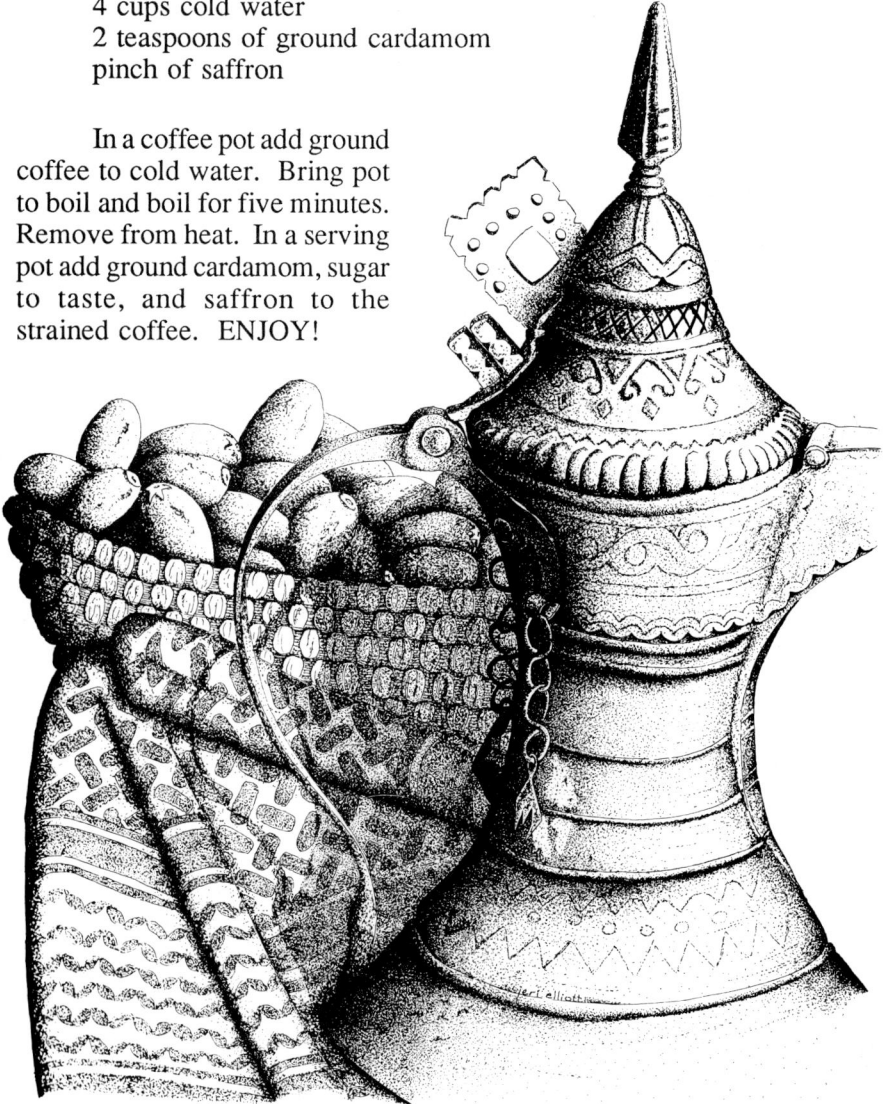

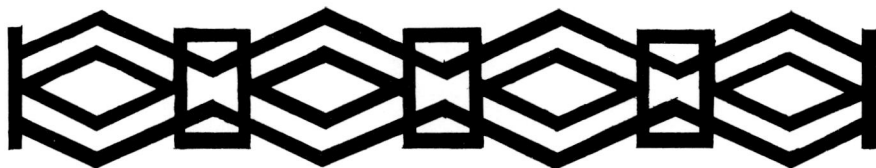

ARAB COFFEE

An aspect of Arab life that impresses one the most is hospitality and this is greatly expressed with 'gahwa'. Serving freshly brewed gahwa, or coffee to guests is an age old custom, whether the gathering is business or social, in an air-conditioned office or a bedouin tent. Sugary tea, no milk, and cold drinks are also offered, along with dates or sweets. It is always polite to accept at least one cup of gahwa from your host, who has the privilege of always pouring. When you are finished a simple little jiggle of your cup from side to side indicates that you are finished. Hold your empty cup out for more and your generous host will continue to fill it up. A polite custom when drinking gahwa at a Saudi home is to accept an odd number of cups, one, three or five, for example. The Arab gahwa is served in small handleless cups, which are only half-filled, from a 'dellah' or Arab coffee pot, that is fashioned in either copper, brass or silver by craftsmen who stamp their work similar to that of gold and silver hallmarking. Typical characteristics of these beautiful coffeepots include the slender spout, the narrow neck, the rotund base, and often intricate designs worked into the metal. The coffee pot is always present, though nowadays gahwa is likely to be prepared early in the day and kept hot in a vacuum flask ready for any visitor who might drop in.

Green coffee beans are roasted and then pounded into a fine powder by mortar and pestle. Saudis do not roast their coffee beans as long as the Lebanese so the Saudi coffee is lighter in color. You can purchase coffee beans in the souq to roast and grind yourself or you can buy ready-made.

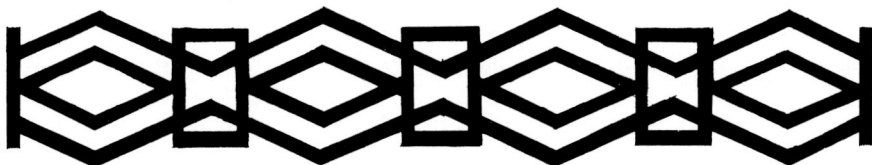

THE SOUQ

An essential feature of every Arab town is the 'souq' or market place. Distinctive to the souq are the adjacent stalls selling similar goods creating smaller sub-souqs such as the gold souq, an impressive sight — window after window abounding in glittering bangles and elaborately worked necklaces; or the material souq where the textile merchants peddle their colorful cloth side by side. You will see store after store selling watches or a block of stores marketing housewares, all grouped together. As you wander through the narrow lanes a variety of robust odors tempt your senses — cardamom, an aromatic seed popular for flavoring sweets, beverages, curries and rice dishes; whole cloves; ginger; and the powerful aroma of curry powder; all mingle with other savory spices from the orient abounding in heaps at the spice stalls within the souq.   Merchants sit cross-legged with their goods piled high around them, their bins overflowing with these exotic herbs and spices.

The vegetable markets display a rainbow of fruits and vegetables imported from all over the world. "Come on in, good prices for you," beckon you from stall to stall. There are locksmiths, carpet and brass merchants, carpenters and various craftsmen in the souq.

Sometimes these souqs are located amid the ground levels of buildings sitting tightly together, the smells and sounds travelling down the narrow corridors between these buildings, the streets shadowed by their multi-story heights. Other souqs, even within the same towns, are located in open air markets, temporary stalls offering, as a sample, perfumes, tobacco leaves and clothes for their children.

Although the souqs have changed little in the smaller villages, oil wealth and the age of modernization is pervading the traditional ways of Arab market life. There is a bustling mixture of old and new existing side by side, in the larger cities. We see hi-fi's and henna, camels and cassettes along with cafes that sell their fast-food and the coffee houses where the Arab men sip gahwa and smoke the sheeshah.

MISWAK

As you wander along the Arabian market streets you may see an Arab sitting crossed-leg on a cloth with a small pile of twigs in front of him. Business looks good! Selling sticks?

The sticks come from the arak tree, grown mainly around Taif, and are used to clean the teeth — the sticks are toothbrushes! Saudis use the miswak on their teeth not only because university studies in the Kingdom have shown the twigs to be healthy for the gums and teeth but because the Prophet Mohammed used sticks from the Arak tree to cleanse his teeth. If you are feeling adventurous enough to try one, I would recommend purchasing the small tender twigs as they are much softer on the gums.

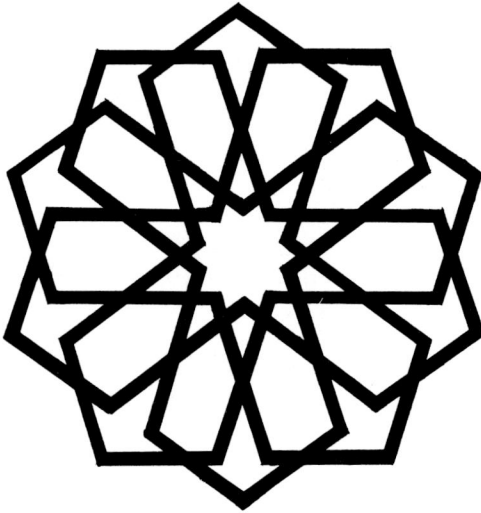

ISLAMIC ART

The art of the Arabian peninsula grew out of the Islamic way of life creating a distinctive traditional Arab art. Interpretations of the Prophet Mohammed's sayings forbade portrayals of people or animals in religious art or elsewhere. So instead Arabia adopted the style of Muslim occupied lands, with the Islamic influence adding symmetry and a sense of visual rhythm grown out of their interest in astronomy and mathematics. As a result designs seen throughout the desert Kingdom rely on abstract and mathematical forms such as the one drawn here. Artistic renderings of Quranic verses done in calligraphy designs are typical of Arab art. Their abstract art designs are often seen decorating buildings, such as mosques. Islamic art style is also displayed in the typical Arab craft work, such as their handwoven rugs, textiles and in pottery and metalwork designs.

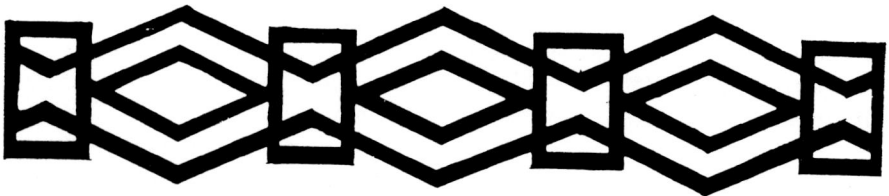

DID YOU KNOW THAT . . .
King Solomon's mine of ancient Arabia was not a myth, and was in fact reopened in 1939. It was worked for its gold and silver deposits but was closed again in 1954 as it was no longer profitable.

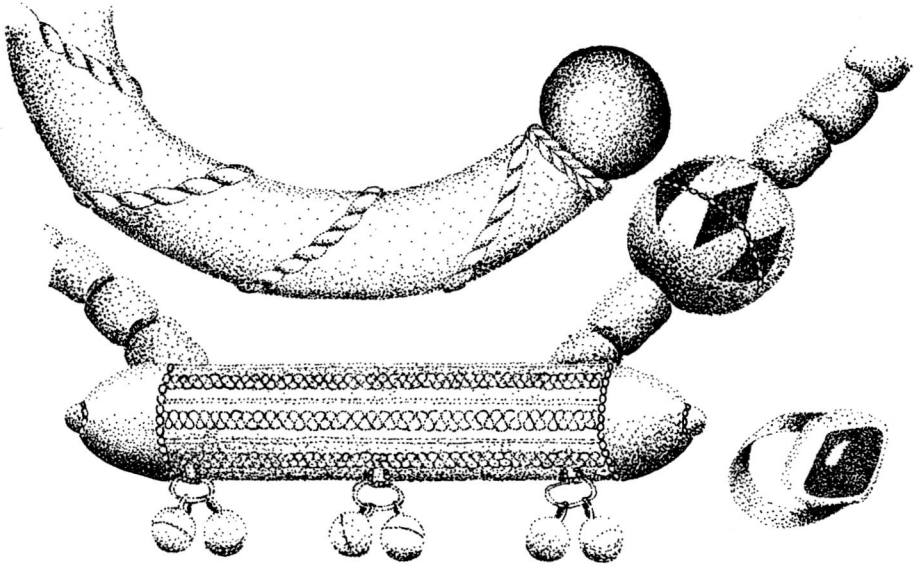

BEDOUIN JEWELRY

Distinctive from any other jewelry the bedouin's jewelry is both impressive and imposing. The bold, massive designs are usually fashioned in a silver based alloy. Intricate designs are fashioned in filigree, along with balls, bells, links and solid meshes of polished silver. The silver is often studded with amber, coral, pearls, garnets, agate or turquoise. Bedouin jewelry is to be treasured and is always made in a variety of qualities so both the rich and the poor can afford to possess the same traditional styles.

Each bedouin tribe had its own weavers, leather workers, coppersmiths and silversmiths. The silversmiths were the makers of this traditional bedouin jewelry which today is in danger of being lost forever. Bedouin jewelry is still being made but the number of silversmiths has diminished and so has the quality of workmanship.

When a bedouin bride marries she receives only new ornaments and may be heavily adorned with headpieces, collar-like necklaces, bracelets, bangles and belts. When a women dies all of her remaining jewelry is sold and often melted down. It is a wonder that old pieces are still around today after successfully spanning 2000 years.

THE ARABIAN DAGGER

In earlier times the crescent-shaped scabbards, or 'jambiyya,' worn by the bedouin tribesmen were fashioned by the tribes' silversmiths. Jambiyya comes from the root word 'jam' which means "side,"— 'something on the side.' The curved dagger with its sheath was a weapon worn by most males in the region until the second quarter of this century. It is reputed that the Arabian style knife was designed with a short curve so the wearer would avoid being stabbed while sitting or horse riding. It was customary for a man to regard himself as properly dressed only after he had donned his sheathed dagger and perhaps a rifle. Today it is used for ceremonial purposes only.

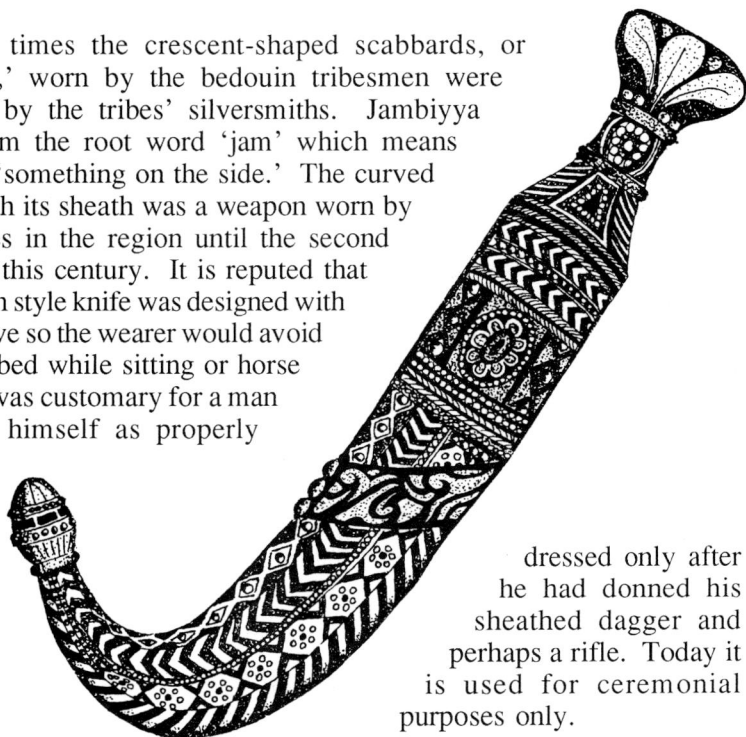

THE ARABIC LANGUAGE

"The Language Chosen by God for his Final Revelation."
—Mohammed the Prophet and his followers

Arabic is a poetic Semitic language spoken in 21 countries, however dialects vary from country to country whereby, for example, a Moroccan Arab would not understand an Iraqi's language. Classical Arabic, the language of the Quran, is today used occasionally in writing but rarely in speech. However, it is important to note here that when two Arabs are unable to understand each other's native dialects the universal Arabic of the Quran binds these two Muslims and may enable them to communicate. A standardized modern Arabic is used for newspapers, conversing and television.

Arabic is written in a flowing cursive style from right to left. The alphabet is comprised of 28 letters, all consonants, vowels being expressed either by positioned points or, in some cases, by insertion of the letters 'alif,' 'waw,' and 'yah' in positions where they would not otherwise occur, thereby representing the long **a, u** and **i** respectively. Arabic letters take different shapes depending on the occurrence — alone, the final, middle or initial position of a word.

Due to the foreign appearance of written Arabic and its guttural sounds, most Westerners may assume it is a difficult language to learn, however conversational Arabic is relatively easy to learn to speak and the people of Arabia enjoy it when a foreigner makes the effort to speak their language, despite the newcomer's mistakes, or misplacement of words.

Throughout the Middle East translations for certain words will vary. Notice some of the similarity in some words to the western world's language — for example 'laymun' for lemon and the Spanish words 'bantalone' and 'khamees' for pants and shirt (two words the Arabs borrowed in the 13th century when the Moors conquered Spain).

Following is a list of useful words and phrases to get newcomers started.

GREETINGS
Hello and welcome .... Assalam alaykum
Hello (response) .... Waalaykum assalam
Hello (informal) .... Marhaba
Good morning .... Sabah al khair
Good morning (response) .... Sabah anoor
Good evening .... Masa al khair
Welcome .... Ahlan Wasahlan
Goodbye .... Fi amanillah
Goodbye (response) .... Ma'asalama
How are you? .... Kaif Halek?
Fine thank you .... Al hamdulillah

USEFUL WORDS AND PHRASES
please .... minfadlak
get well soon .... salamtek
thank you .... shukran
you're welcome .... afwan
no .... la
yes .... na'am
after you .... tafadhal
God willing .... enshalah
no problem .... ma fi mushkilla
never mind .... ma alaysh
sorry; excuse me .... assif
my name is . . . . ismi . . . .
I have . . . . indi . . . .
enough; only .... bes
stop .... kef
by foot .... meshi

car	sayara	4	araba'a
same thing	nefs ashay	5	khamsa
same place	nefs al macon	6	sitta
new	jadeed	7	saba'a
letter	resalah	8	thamania
magazine	majelleh	9	tisa'a
newspaper	jereedeh	10	ashra
perhaps	yumkin	11	ahdasher
must	lazim	12	ethnasher
beautiful (f)	jameel or helwah	13	thalathatasher
beautiful (m)	helu	14	arabatasher
in my hand	fi yady	15	khamstasher
north	shamal	16	sittasher
south	janub	17	sabatasher
east	shark	18	thaminatasher
west	gharb	19	tisatasher
window	nafizah	20	ashreen
hot	har	30	thalatheen
cold	barid	40	arba'een
friend	sadeek	50	khamseen
money	feluus	60	siteen
small	seghira(f);	70	saba'een
	saghir (m)	80	thamaneen
big	kabira (f);	90	tiseen
	kabir (m)	100	miya
or	ao	1000	alf
and	wa		
bathroom	hammam		

NUMERALS

0	sifr
1	wahed
2	ithnayn
3	thalatha

sun	shems
weather	aljow
much; many	wajid; katheer
very	kilish
a little	shwayya; galeel
book	khitab
door	baab
sick	mareed
half	nisf; nus
finish	khalas

TIME

today	al yom
tomorrow	bukra
yesterday	ams
year	sana
week	isbu
month	shahar
day before yesterday	awal ams
day after tomorrow	ba'ad bukra
everyday	kul yom
always	diamon
later; after	badain
before	gabl
again	marathania
now	al hain

QUESTIONS

where	wayn
who	man
what	maza
how many	kam
how much	bi kam
what do you want	matha tareed
when	mita
why	lesh
which	aiy

DAYS OF THE WEEK

Saturday	yom assabt
Sunday	yom alahad
Monday	yom alithnain
Tuesday	yom althalatha
Wednesday	yom alarba'a
Thursday	yom al khamees
Friday	yom al juma

THE FAMILY

boy	walad
girl	bint
father	abu or ab
mother	um
husband	zaoj
wife	zawja
married	mutezoweej
son of	ibn

FOOD

food	akl
bread	khubz
coffee	gahwa
milk	haleeb
water	ma'a
tea	shii
sugar	sukkar
orange	burtukal
banana	moz
carrots	karaz
grapes	enab
cucumber	oteruh; khyar
apple	tofah

strawberry	toot
onion	basal
potato	alow
tomato	tamatin
watermelon	battikn
lemon	laymun
grapefruit	karafoot
pear	anjas
chicken	dejudge
fish	samak
rice	roz
meat	le'ham
salad	salad

COLORS

color	lon
red	ahmar
yellow	asfar
blue	asraq
green	akhdar
brown	buni
black	aswad
white	abyad
pink	wardi
gold	dahabi
silver	fiddi

CLOTHES

pants	bantalone
shirt	khamees for m.
blouse	bloosa for f.
shoes	juti
sandals	naal
dress	fustan

PLACES

airport	matar
hotel	funduq
hospital	mustashfa
market	souq
house	bait
work	amal; shughul
restaurant	mataam
sea	bahar

AL DERWAHZA

A unique characteristic of Arab architecture is the Arab door, or 'derwahza' (a word of Persian origin). These old doors are made from wood usually imported from India. The wood is carved in elaborate designs and many old doors are stained with bright natural colorings. Brass or iron strips with studs help support the vertical slats of wood. Other decorative additions might include brass plates cut in a variety of geometrical shapes, along with locks and latches designed locally. The large double doors open in the middle but are used only when large articles must be carried inside the home. Otherwise the smaller door that is inset in one side of the double doors is used for everyday passage.

WINDTOWERS

Before electricity and air-conditioning in the torrid desert, Arab homes were designed to create cool living conditions and this often included perforated windows through which sunlight only filters in and windtowers or windcatchers. As an addition to homes, the windtower is designed to catch the wind from any direction and, acting like a flue, direct the breeze down into the living spaces through opened doors below. During its passage through the tower the breeze accelerates due to a pulling down-draft and also loses most of its heat. This cool air circulates through the house reducing the interior temp-erature. Even when there is no breeze a down-draft is created when the hot ambient air entering the tower is cooled. The windtower also works to cool the home in another way, by allowing rising hot air to escape through the towers' upper openings. Although windtowers are still seen throughout the Middle East on older dwellings, they are no longer a part of the modern homes being built today.

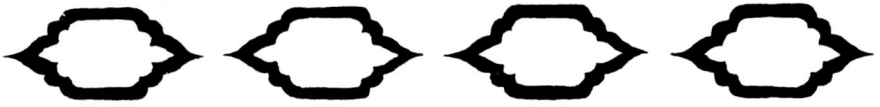

EATING ARABIC STYLE

A traditional Arab meal is arranged on a cloth or mat that is spread on the floor with separate dishes and platters of food, plates and cutlery. In a bedouin tent you would perhaps experience eating from one large platter using the fingers of the right hand only to roll up balls of rice and pull tender pieces of meat from the cooked lamb to pop in your mouth. The left hand should not touch the food, nor should you pass anything to your fellow diners with the left hand. As you sit upon the floor enjoying your meal keep the soles of your feet from facing anyone; that would be extremely offensive. Before and after a meal, coffee and tea are served. In a bedouin's tent great ceremony is made of the coffee ritual. Beans are roasted over an open fire and pounded into a fine powder in a mortar and pestle. Boiled in water and flavored with cardamom, Arab coffee is then served in tiny handleless cups.

Before an Arab eats it is necessary to say 'bismallah,' (in the name of God). When finished the meal he will say 'al hamdullillah,' (to God be thankful). The main dish of the meal is usually lamb, the staple meat of the Middle East. However, beef, chicken, or fish caught in the gulf waters might also be served. Rice is always present whether cooked on its own with Arab spices or cooked with the meat. Basmati rice seems to be the most popular in this region, basmati needs washing and the tiny stones removed.

A variety of side dishes and salads are served dressed simply with vinegar and fresh lemon juice. Bowls of yogurt are offered in abundance along with stacks of hot Arab flat bread. The men will eat in a separate room from the women and usually first. Arab hospitality and a feeling of welcome is abounding and there is always more than enough food served to the guests.

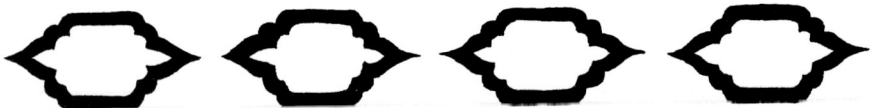

THE LUNAR CALENDAR

The Islamic calendar is based on the moon's 30 day phases — from new moon to new moon there is an interval of 29 days, 12 hours, 44 minutes and 2.78 seconds. This lunar year is 354 days long, 11 days short of the solar year or Gregorian calendar used by the majority of the world's countries. As a result the Islamic religious festivals and months run through all the seasons of the year three times per century, thus their days slip back 11 days earlier each year. About every 3 years to adjust an overlap in the months an extra day is added, making a 'leap' year of 355 days.

Each month begins with the first appearance of the lunar crescent (making actual dates uncertain) and since this can best be observed in the evening, the day begins at sunset.

Year 1 of the Islamic calendar is the year that the Prophet Mohammed migrated (hijra) to Medina from Makka to spread the word of Islam — July 622 a.d. — hence the name "Hijriya" calendar. Dates during the Islamic era are indicated by a.h. (anno hijira).

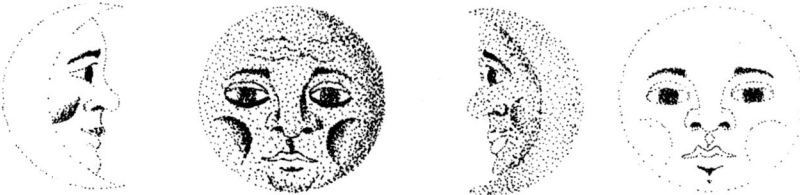

Listed here are the 12 Hijriya months —

1st   Muharram (Ashoora celebrated)
2nd   Safar
3rd   Rabi al Awwal
4th   Rabi ath Thani
5th   Jumada al Ula
6th   Jumada al Akhirah
7th   Rajab
8th   Shaban
9th   Ramadan (month of fasting)
10th Shawwal
11th Dhu al Qadah
12th Dhu al Hijjah (pilgrimage to Makka)

CELEBRATED DAYS

Eid al-Fitr — Festival following the End of Fasting. The first three days of Shawwal, the month that follows the fasting month of Ramadan, are a celebration of breaking fast. This is a time of joy and rejoicing, children receive presents such as new clothes, toys or sweets and alms are distributed. Eid al-Adha — Feast of the Sacrifice. This is a three day holiday that occurs after the hajj, the 10th through the 12th during the month of Dhu al Hijjah. Eid al-Adha commemorates God's sparing Ibrahim's sacrifice of his son. The feast, culminating the pilgrimage, is accompanied by gift-giving, distribution of food, and family gatherings, whether in Makka or at home.

WINDS

'Shamal' means north and describes the seasonal windstorms of Arabia which generally come from that direction, north. During the winter the shamal winds come with the cooler weather dropping the temperature even lower. During the summer a breeze would normally be welcomed, but the shamal winds blow hot gusts, serving only to increase the uncomfortable heat. The sky turns dark as the winds hasten their intensity gathering sand along the way and flinging it skyward. A shamal can blow and kick up the sand for days. During humid days the sand is trapped in the moisture drops in the atmosphere creating an eerie orange tinted blanket over the desert and its inhabitants. The weather of this desert kingdom varies greatly throughout the year from intense heat, humid coastal areas, dry central plains, to freezing winter temperatures in the mountains and sparse rainfall in most areas while still other areas receive torrential rains creating floods. The arid desert image is deceiving to those not accustomed to its extreme diversities.

KOHL

Kohl is the black powder used by Arab and Asian women to enhance the beauty of their eyes. The best kohl is produced in India and in the Arabian peninsula. The soot of burnt almonds, benzoin and incense is collected to form the kohl powder. The inside of the upper and lower edges of the eyelids are darkened by kohl sticks made from ivory, wood or metal. The powder is stored in small ornate bottles made from glass or metal.

Arabs not only use kohl as a cosmetic, but as a medicine for infected eyes. Babies' eyes are even painted with kohl to protect them from infections and also against the glare of the sun.

CAMEL RACING

A camel race is an exciting spectacle, the camels' ungainly canter, the flying dust, and the riders amazingly staying atop. Races are either organized on a course track similar to horse racing tracks or the camels and their riders, usually young boys, thunder across an open stretch of sand. Breeding of lightweight camels plays an important role here and the camel driver is an expert with his camels. You do not want to miss a chance to see a camel race.

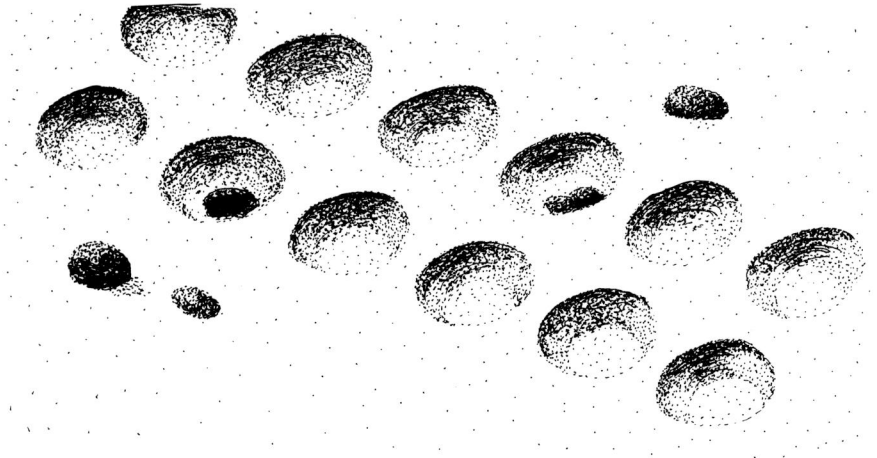

MANCALA

Mancala refers to games originated with Stone Age African tribes, yet display all the mathematical complexity of the computer age. Bedouins play a certain form of mancala in sand indentations using stones or camel dung as the playing pieces. Players pick up pieces from a pit and move them into other pits. The object of the game, which varies according to the game played, usually involves capturing the most pieces.

THE ARABIAN HORSE

A horse of timeless beauty, the Arabian grew to its faultless splendor over centuries of carefully controlled breeding practices by the bedouin tribes. In the 7th century the Arabian horse provided

speedy transport during the Islamic conquests and bedouin raids. However, the horse could not endure the long harsh desert journeys like the camel, so instead became a status symbol of the wealthy. The distinctive characteristics of the Arabian include a small head, large eyes, flaring nostrils, short sleek back, strong slender legs and great stamina.

The swiftness and gracefulness has produced an enduring racehorse. Although the Arabians are usually reddish-brown, grey and white ones are highly valued. It is reputed that the Prophet Mohammed owned 15 mares during his lifetime. In the Quran it is written that every man shall revere his horse.

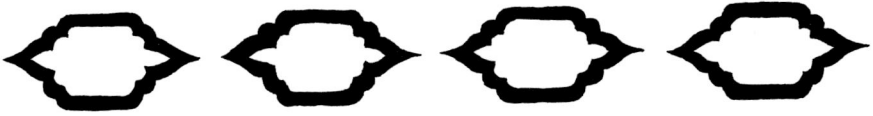

DHOWS

The high-masted dhow, now diesel powered, is a sea-going vessel. This ancient craft, that has been used in the Arabian and East African coastal trade for over 2000 years, has hardly changed its design at all over the centuries. Even the ancient building methods, used until recent years, were unchanged. Traditionally the dhow is built without nails, and without using mechanized instruments, however modern vessels do have nails and a minority of the builders use electric drills. Wood used to build dhows is often imported from India — such as teak, mangrove, and acacia.

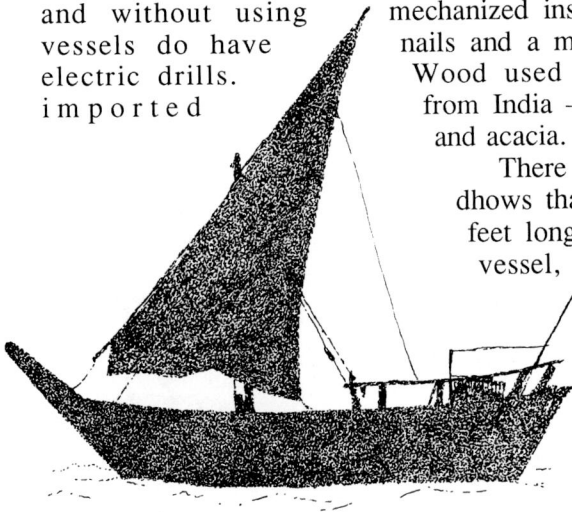

There are many different types of dhows that range in length from six feet long, the small inshore fishing vessel, to the larger ocean going vessels. The dhow goes by a variety of names depending on its use — for fishing, cargo, or pearl diving for example — 'baggola,' 'boom,' 'sambuk,' and 'shuui.'

FALCONS

In a seemingly lifeless desert the Arabs hunt small prey with their falcons; the bedouin do so to catch meat for their meals and others for the sport. These quick and agile hunter-birds are extremely successful in hunting their prey.

In 1977 King Khalid banned the use of firearms within the Kingdom, thus the serious sport of falconry became one of the only forms of hunting permitted. Prince Khalid bin Faisal has pioneered a farm for falcons in the Abha area of Saudi Arabia. Falcon training and breeding at this farm will preserve the falcon's future in Saudi Arabia.

There are skilled falconers located throughout the Kingdom. Their skill begins the moment a young bird is taken from its nest. The small

bird's eyes are stitched shut when caught. The trainer keeps the sightless bird with him night and day for a month. The falcon becomes attuned to his surroundings, the smells, the sounds, his master's voice. The trainer and only the trainer feeds the bird who trusts his master. A friendship grows out of this unique training.

The stitches on the eye lids are later removed, but the training and companionship continues. The falcon, having always depended on his food from his master, is now made to go hungry for a few days, to prepare for additional training. A long cord is attached to the falcon's leg and he is allowed to fly. The bird's master tempts the bird back to his arm with a piece of raw meat. Eventually the bird learns to return by his master's call alone. Additional training stages include accustoming the bird to leather leg straps and a blinding hood. The hood is removed prior to the hunt. During hunting the falcon flies free ready to kill. Due to the bonding trust the falcon always returns to perch on his master's arm.

A story was recounted to me by an acquaintance whose uncle went to the desert with his falcon, but only the bird returned to the camp. The family discovered the bird in its travel box where he had been trained to return. The family hunted for the man justly concerned at the bird's solo return. Unfortunately the man was found dead but he was retrieved. In another story, an Arab man was bit by a snake while his bird was in flight. The bird returned to the camp and made outward flying motions which prompted the men from the camp to search for the bird's master. They found him, sick but alive. The falcon had saved his life.

DATES—FRUITS OF ARABIA

Within the desert gardens of the arid sands, often guarded by tall towers, grow the sturdy palms fed by unseen underground water. Without the palm there would be no oases development; most vegetation in an oasis can survive only in the presence of the palm. The fruit of the palm is the date, or 'tamr' and is the chief crop of the oasis. In fact, before the production of oil in the 1930's much of Saudi Arabia's revenue was from the export of dates. The al-Hasa oases of the eastern province form the core of the date industry with some of the palms having produced fruit for over a hundred years. There are over 65 varieties grown and the Arabs have given these delicate dates some suitable poetic names, such as "Red Sugar," "Bride's Finger," "Mother of Perfume," and "Pure Daughter," to offer the translation of only a few.

To speak of dates is to speak of the life of the Arabic people, for from the carefully monitored growth, to harvesting, to marketing, to eating — all the people of Arabia are included. Harvesting of the date goes on over a variety of months depending on the type of date desired. Dates picked during May and June are in the early ripeness or 'bisr' stage and are still firm. The next stage, 'rutab,' produces semi-ripe dates and lasts until September. The final stage after September, 'tamr,' is when the dates are the most sweet, my favorite. This is a good time to use the dates to cook delicious Arab delicacies. At the heart of any Arab social occasion, big or small, you will always see dates.

THE CAMEL

When Saudi Arabia is mentioned oil, sand, and camels immediately come to mind, and although there is much more to Saudi Arabia, the camel has had an important role in the shaping of this desert peninsula making desert travel possible.

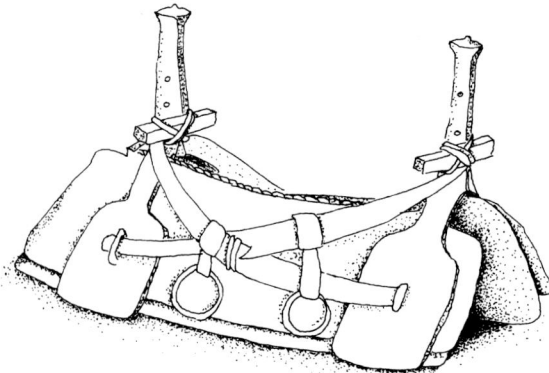

The one humped camel is called a dromedary or Arabian camel. The camel's feet are flat, broad leathery pads that prevent the animal from sinking into the sand. There are similar

44

'A NEW MOTHER'

patches of dry, hard skin on the chest and legs to protect the camel when its body must bear its weight in a resting position or rising position. When walking, the camel moves both feet on one side of the body, then both on the other, causing the body to 'roll' while walking. The camel is sometimes called the "ship of the desert," being the mode of transport across this arid sea of sand.

The bedouin travellers ride the female camels which also provide fresh milk for their tribes. The male camels are also a beast of burden, carrying enormous loads, up to 1000 pounds, although their average baggage load in a caravan is about 400 pounds. Every night the goods are unloaded and some of the camels have their front legs hobbled together with leather thongs to prevent them from wandering.

The camel was initially domesticated by the Arabian people it is said before 1300 BC, as a dairy animal and then discovered to be an invaluable carrier for caravans crossing the hot desert sands. It was the northern bedouin who developed a saddle for the camel enabling them to sit securely over the camel's hump, not behind it like the young riders sit during a camel race. The bedouin were true masters of the camel and expert riders. The camel was essential for survival in the desert interior, and has even been introduced into the desert regions of Australia.

Many stories are told about the camel's ability to store water in its hump. The camel does not store water, but actually stores fat there to use during the dry season when food is scarce. As the camel's body uses the fat for food, the hump gets smaller and flabby. A camel can go three days without water, five days if necessary. The camel is able to withstand a loss of about a third of his body fluid without danger. When water is readily available, the camel can drink great quantities at a time, up to 15 gallons. In the desert, camels depend on man for most of their food, but will eat grass and leaves that they can find. Because they have a double row of eyelashes and can close their nostrils completely, camels can stand or travel in sandstorms.

Camels provide food, clothing, leather, and fuel for man. Besides drinking the camel's milk, desert dwellers sometimes pour it into a leather pouch and let it sour, they then make cheese, or bread made of sour milk and flour. The camel's hair can be woven into cloth for tents and clothing and dung is used for fuel. Wealth is often determined by the number of camels a man owns. In some tribes, camels are traded instead of money for dowries. The beast has a surly disposition and is often unpredictable or stubborn, even dangerous.

Camels, whose life expectancy is about 25 years, can be very expensive, from SR 500 (NZ$250) to SR 6000 (NZ$3000) each, depending on the camel's age, sex and purpose — a racing camel, for example, would be in the higher price bracket. A female camel can breed every second year and usually gives birth to a single calf.

Nose to tail the male pack animals continue to cross the desert on centuries-old caravan routes while the females graze on the desert scrub like roaming sheep.

RECIPES
FROM THE
ARAB KITCHEN

BAHARAT

(ARABIC MIXED SPICES; ALSO CALLED 'BJAR')

This mixture of spices used in Arab dishes can be purchased ready made at an Arab grocery store. Or you can make it yourself by blending together the following spices.

Makes nearly 3 cups of baharat:
1/3 cup black pepper
1/4 cup coriander powder
1/5 cup cinnamon
1/5 cup cloves
1/3 cup cumin
2 teaspoons ground cardamom
1/4 cup ground nutmeg
1/2 cup ground paprika
1/3 cup curry
1/5 cup ground dried limes
Store in a tightly sealed spice jar.

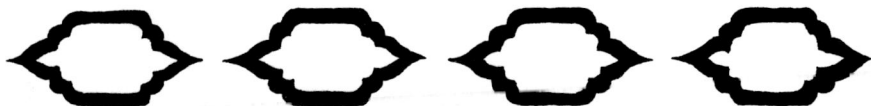

KIBBEH

(DEEP FRIED MINCED LAMB AND BURGHUL)

Kibbeh mixture:
500 grams minced lamb
2 cups burghul, soaked in water for 10 minutes, drained
and squeeze out excess water
1 finely chopped onion
1 clove garlic, crushed
1 tsp. allspice
salt and pepper

Stuffing:
1 1/2 tbls. olive oil
2 tbls. pine kernels
1 small onion, finely chopped
125 grams minced lamb
1/8 tsp. allspice
1/2 tsp. salt

Saute stuffing ingredients over moderate heat until golden
brown and then set aside. In bowl knead together kibbeh
mixture ingredients. Wet hands with cold water. Take a small
lump of kibbeh mixture, size of an egg, into your left hand.
Make an indent in the center with the index finger of your
right hand. With the left hand work the meat around the index
finger in a long hollow torpedo shape — if cracks form use a
moistened finger to repair. Fill the shell with a tablespoon of
the stuffing mixture. Close the opening by wetting the rim in
cold water and pressing together. Pat and smooth. Deep fry
in oil until they are a rich dark brown color. Drain. May be
served hot or cold.

Sometimes the outer kibbeh shell is made with seasoned
cracked wheat alone. Kibbeh meat mixture can be layered in
a casserole dish with the stuffing mixture and baked in the
oven at 180°C (350° F). for 30 minutes.

KOUSA MAHSHI

(STUFFED ZUCCHINI WITH TOMATO SAUCE)

8 to 10 small zucchini
500 grams ground beef or lamb
2/3 cup uncooked rice washed and drained
salt and pepper to taste

1/2 tsp. ground allspice or mixed spices (see recipe index for baharat)
Clean the zucchini under cold water and pat dry. Cut about one inch off
the stem ends. Carefully funnel out the center of each. To make the
stuffing combine ground meat, rice, salt, pepper, and allspice. Spoon
stuffing into hollowed out zucchini and shake stuffing down. Fill the
squash 3/4 full to prevent bursting when the rice expands.

Sauce:
1 cup finely chopped onions
1 cup chopped tomatoes
1 small can tomato paste
salt and pepper to taste
1 tsp. allspice or baharat

Fry onions in one tablespoon of oil until golden then add tomatoes, salt,
pepper, and baharat, stir. Add tomato paste and stir. Add zucchini and
enough boiling water to cover the zucchini. Bring to a boil and then cover
and cook on low to medium low heat for 45 minutes. Delicious!

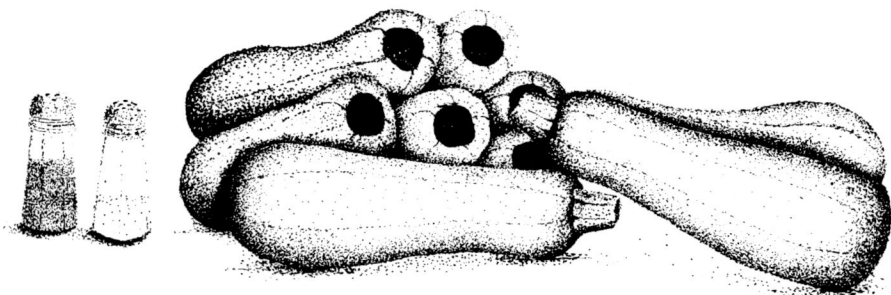

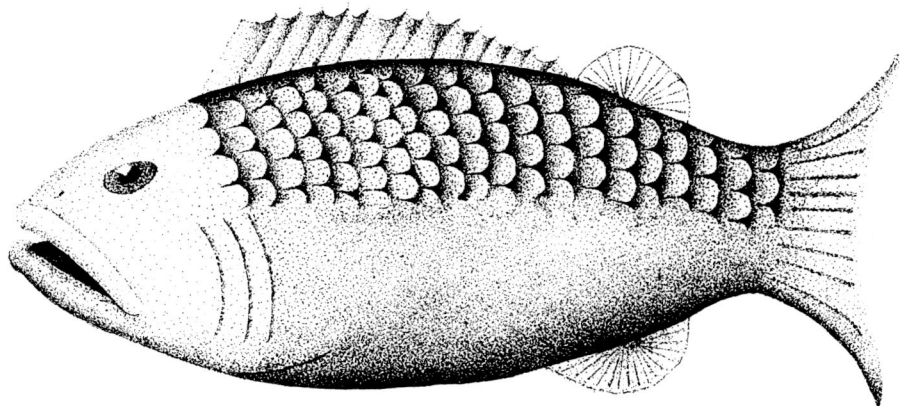

HAMOUR MAHSHI

(STUFFED GROUPER)

1 whole hamour (1 1/2 kilos)
2 onions (sliced in semicircles)
2 cloves garlic crushed
1/2 cup coriander chopped
1 1/2 cups chopped tomatoes
1 cup chopped green pepper
1 cup olive oil
2 tsps. baharat (see recipe index)
1/2 cup lemon juice

To prepare fish — cut head off partially just behind the gills (so it can be replaced to appear whole). Remove fins and entrails. Cut 3 diagonal slashes on both sides of the fish and rub with some of the garlic, spices, and lemon juice.

Mix together tomatoes, peppers, coriander, onions, garlic and mixed spices. In a separate bowl blend lemon and oil until thick. Pour half of this into the onion mixture and stir.

Brush the bottom of a large baking dish with some of the oil mixture. Spoon in a third of the onion mixture, stuff the fish with another third of the onion mixture and place in the dish. Top off with the remaining onion mixture. Pour the rest of the lemon/oil mixture into the baking dish and cover with foil. Bake at 180°C (350°F) for 40 minutes. Uncover and cook for 20 minutes more.

51

BARIYANI

(LAMB WITH RICE)

1 1/2 kilos lamb shoulder or leg
2 potatoes peeled and cut into cubes
1 green pepper chopped
3 onions chopped
3 tsps. baharat (see recipe index)
2 cloves garlic crushed
1/2 cup chopped coriander
4 cloves
2 cinnamon sticks
5 cardamom seeds
2 bay leaves
1/2 cup oil
1 tsp. saffron
1/3 cup rose water
4 cups rice (basmati rice)
1 cup yogurt
2 tsps. salt

In a small glass mix the rose water and saffron with 1/3 cup of hot water. Let sit to allow the color to come out.

In a large container add raw meat, onions, peppers, potatoes, coriander, baharat, yogurt, bay leaves, garlic, and half the oil. Mix well and set aside.

In a large pot bring 4 cups of water and salt to taste to a boil, add rice. Stir and cook until only half-done. Drain out excess water. Do not rinse. In the same large pot (after emptying) add 2 tablespoons of oil and 2 cups of drained rice. Flatten rice evenly in pot. Add the meat mixture and the remaining ingredients. Add 3 teaspoons of the rose water mixture. Add the remaining rice breaking up lumps if they form. Top off with the rose water mixture and the rest of the oil. Cover tightly and cook over medium-low heat for 2 to 3 hours until done.

(Try this recipe with chicken.)

BAMYA

(OKRA AND LAMB)

This Arab dish is great for any leftover meat.

500 grams okra
2 large tomatoes, chopped
1 tbls. fresh mint, chopped
500 grams cubed lamb
1 large onion, chopped
1 tbls. chopped fresh parsley
3 or 4 crushed garlic cloves (optional)
1 small can tomato paste
juice from one lemon
salt and pepper to taste

Wash okra and remove stems sparingly, so pods will not burst while cooking. Combine okra in a bowl with the lemon juice, let stand. In large pot cook onions in oil until golden. Add meat, cook until brown. Add tomatoes, parsley, garlic, and seasoning. Add 2 cups of boiling water and tomato paste. Drain the okra and add to the pot, if necessary add enough boiling water so okra is covered. Return to a boil, cover tightly and simmer for 2 hours.

Serves 6 to 8.

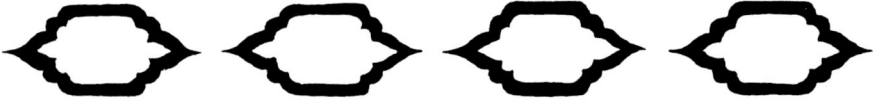

KABSA

(A TRADITIONAL DISH OF RICE AND MEAT)

2 large onions, chopped
1/2 cup oil
1 tbls. baharat (see recipe index)
1 tsp. turmeric
1 1/2 kilo lamb shoulder
        cut into 6 pieces or any other cut of lamb
2 cups fresh tomatoes chopped
2 cloves garlic
2 whole cloves
1 tsp. black lime powder
1 stick cinnamon
4 cardamom seeds
4 1/2 cups water
1/2 cup chopped coriander
2 cups basmati rice
salt to taste

In large pot fry onion with oil. Add cloves, cinnamon and cardamom. Fry for 2 minutes. Add mixed spices, turmeric, garlic, and coriander. Cook for 5 minutes. Add meat and brown. Add tomatoes, lime and salt. Cook 5 to 10 minutes. Add water, cover and simmer for 2 to 2 1/2 hours, until meat is tender.

Pick over basmati rice for stones if necessary and place in a bowl to wash thoroughly. Drain and stir into the meat. Reduce heat and cover tightly. Simmer for 20 minutes stirring once or twice during cooking. When cooked pile onto a large platter and sprinkle with pine kernels or sliced almonds.

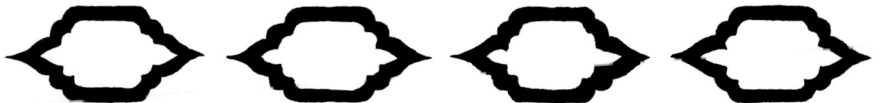

SHISH KEBAB

(GRILLED SKEWERED LAMB)

1 kilo boneless cubed lamb (2 inch squares)
4 tomatoes, quartered
2 green peppers, quartered
2 onions, quartered

Marinade:
2 tbls. olive oil
2 tbls. fresh lemon juice
4 cloves garlic, crushed
salt and pepper
pinch of sugar
pinch of cinnamon
freshly chopped parsley and fennel

Marinate meat in marinade mixture in the refrigerator for at least 4 hours, turning the lamb occasionally. Remove the meat from the marinade and spear onto skewers alternating peppers, tomatoes and onions.

May be grilled in the oven or outside on the barbecue. If cooked in the oven suspend the skewers on the sides of a roasting pan deep enough to allow space below the meat. Grill under the broiler, turning the skewers as necessary until the lamb is cooked to your taste, approximately 10 to 15 minutes. Serve with pilaf.

Serves 4 to 6.

SHAWARMA

(CHARCOAL GRILLED MEAT)

Devouring a savory shawarma will always be a favorite reminder of any visitor's stay in Arabia, their mouth watering at the sight of the sizzling cone of meat. This cone of meat is first marinated in yogurt and seasoning, the sliced meat, (lamb, beef, or chicken) is then placed layer upon layer, put on a spit, and topped off with an onion, tomato, and/or lemon. The spit is placed vertically in front of an open flame. As the meat cooks it is turned. The shawarma chef takes his sharp knife in hand and cuts off paper thin slices of cooked meat which drop into a waiting tray below. The cooked meat, salad and yogurt or hot sauce are placed in the pocket of pita bread or on a long toasted roll. Fantastic!

You can prepare a kilo of shawarma in your own home. Slice a kilo of meat very thin and marinate in the following mixture overnight:

1 cup yogurt
1/2 tsp. black pepper
2 tbls. lemon juice
1/2 tsp. red pepper
3 or 4 cloves minced garlic
1/2 tsp ground mace
1/2 tsp hot pepper sauce
1/2 tsp salt
1 tbls. finely minced onion
1 tbls. vinegar

Place the marinated meat in a barbecue cage and cook over hot coals for 15 minutes. Combine taheeni (sesame oil paste), clove or garlic, lemon juice and parsley until it is of a creamy texture, add water if necessary. Place the cooked meat, sliced tomatoes and onions in pita bread and pour on the taheeni mixture as desired.

ROZ BOHARI

(A TRADITIONAL RICE DISH FROM THE WESTERN REGION OF SAUDI)

1 kilo lamb shoulder or leg cut in pieces
3 cinnamon sticks
4 cloves
1 onion chopped
1 cup shredded carrots
1 cup chickpeas soaked overnight (or from a can)
1 tsp. fresh ground pepper
1 tsp. salt
8 pepper corns
2 tbls. vegetable oil
2 cups rice
1/2 cup chopped tomatoes

In a large pot fry onion, pepper corns, cinnamon and cloves in hot oil until tender. Add meat and brown. Add tomatoes and cook 5 to 10 m i n u t e s. Add ground pepper and salt. Cover and cook for 5 minutes. Add 4 cups of water, cover and cook for 2 hours. Wash rice. When the meat is done add the carrots, chickpeas, and rice. Stir and cook covered on medium heat for 20 minutes.

MALFUF

(CABBAGE ROLLS)

1 large head of cabbage
500 grams of ground beef
1 large onion finely chopped
1 cup parsley finely chopped
1 tsp. pepper
1 tsp. salt
1 egg
1 cup rice
1/3 cup vegetable oil
1 tbls. tomato paste

Core cabbage sparingly and boil in a large pot of water over medium heat until leaves begin to come apart. Remove leaves as they soften and separate. Mix the ground beef with all the ingredients except the tomato paste. Spoon out mixture on each cabbage leaf and roll (tucking sides once). Place rolls in a medium sized pot. Pour on the tomato paste diluted with enough water to cover the rolls. Add 4 tbls. oil, dash of pepper and salt. Cook over medium heat for 1 hour.

PILAF

(STEAMED AND SAUTED RICE)

1 cup long grain rice
2 cloves garlic, crushed
2 tbls. butter
1/2 cup finely chopped onions
1/2 cup mushrooms chopped
1 cup water
1 3/4 cup chicken stock
1/4 cup raisins
salt and pepper to taste

Saute rice, onions, mushrooms, and garlic in hot melted butter in a medium size saucepan until all grains of rice are evenly coated and golden brown. Add water and chicken stock. Bring to a boil, stirring constantly. Cover and simmer for about 20 minutes. Cook until tender and water is absorbed. Season with salt and pepper along with additional melted butter to taste. Plump and soften raisins separately in hot water and drain before adding to the rice. Toss with a fork and cover until ready to serve.

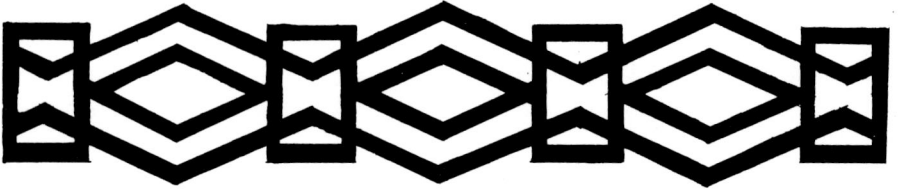

RED LENTIL SOUP

1 1/2 cups small red lentils
1 large onion chopped
1/4 cup oil
4 cloves garlic crushed
1 tsp. baharat (see recipe index)
2 cups chopped tomatoes
2 dried black limes (omit if unable to find)
1/2 cup chopped coriander leaves
6 cups water

Clean lentils under cold water. In a large pot heat oil and fry onions until transparent. Add garlic, mixed spices and coriander. Stir well. Add tomatoes. Cook 5 to 7 minutes. Add lentils, water, salt, and pepper to taste and boil gently until lentils are tender.

TABBOULEH

(PARSLEY, MINT, AND CRACKED WHEAT SALAD)

1 cup fine burghul (cracked wheat)
1 cup finely chopped fresh mint
6 or 7 cups finely chopped large leaf parsley (about 3 bundles)
1 cup finely chopped green onions
1/4 cup finely chopped yellow onions
3/4 cup finely chopped tomatoes
1/2 cup olive oil
1/2 cup fresh lemon juice or per your taste
salt and pepper
dash ground cinnamon

Soften burghul in water for one hour. Using a cheesecloth in a colander drain and press out excess water. In large bowl combine parsley, mint, and onions. In separate bowl whisk together olive oil, lemon juice, salt, pepper, and cinnamon. Just before serving add the parsley mixture to the burghul and tomatoes. Pour the juice mixture over and toss thoroughly with a fork. Garnish with chopped tomatoes and parsley sprigs.

Serves 6 to 8.

(Note — do not use dried herbs with this recipe.)

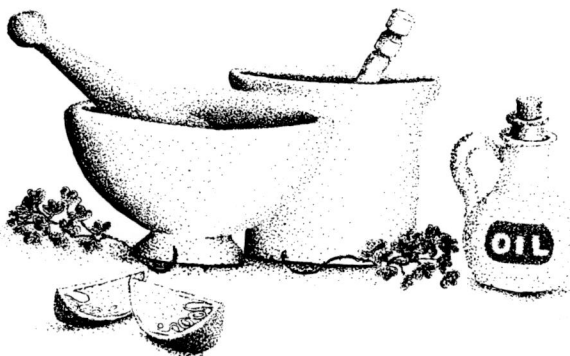

SALAT KHYAR BI LABAN

(SALAD OF CUCUMBER AND YOGURT)

The use of laban in salads is only one of the many ways that this dairy product is used. In the Arab world it is added and cooked with the food, such as hot soups or as a cooking liquid in meat and vegetable dishes. It is also added to rice while it is cooking.

2 1/2 cups yogurt or laban
1 cup peeled chopped cucumbers
3 cloves garlic
1 tsp. dried mint
1 tbls. fresh lemon juice
salt and pepper to taste

Smooth yogurt by stirring with a spoon. Add cucumbers. Work garlic to a paste with salt and add to a spoonful of yogurt before adding to cucumber mixture. Add mint and lemon juice. Serve as a salad with any meal.

(Variations on this dish include using the above mixture as a dressing on a salad of lettuce, tomatoes and onions or simply adding onions and tomatoes to this recipe.)

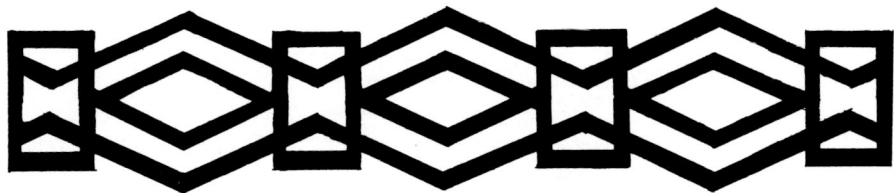

BABA GHANOUSH

(EGGPLANT DIP)

3 large eggplants
3 or 4 cloves garlic, crushed
1/2 cup taheeni (sesame oil)
juice of 3 lemons
1/2 tsp. cumin
2 tbls. chopped parsley
salt

Pierce eggplants in several places with a fork and roast over an open flame (or 4 inches under the broiler) until skin blackens and blisters, turning them as necessary. When cool peel and discard charred skin. Mash the eggplants with a fork and then add crushed garlic and salt. Pound to a smooth, creamy puree. Add the taheeni and lemon juice alternately, blending well between each addition. Add cumin and parsley. Serve as an appetizer with Arab bread quartered.

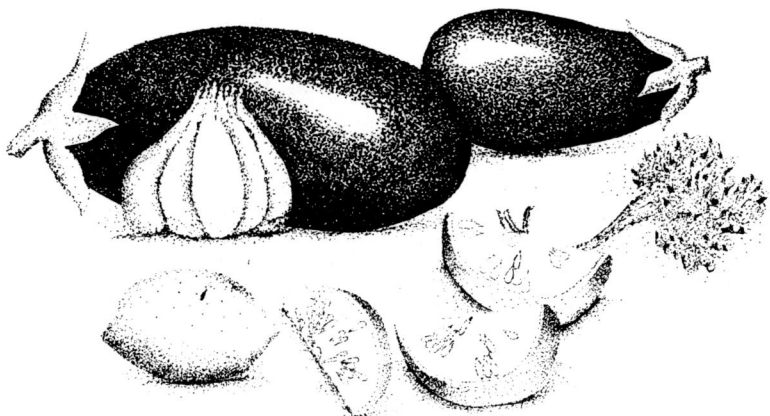

HUMMUS BI TAHEENI

(CHICKPEAS WITH SESAME OIL)

2 1/2 cups dried chick peas, soaked overnight (2 1/2 cans of chick peas
    can be used, no soaking or boiling is necessary)
6 tbls. taheeni (sesame oil)
5 to 6 tbls. fresh lemon juice or per your taste
1 1/2 tsp. salt
2 cloves of garlic or to your taste (pressed or finely chopped)
2 tbls. chopped parsley
1 tbls. olive oil
paprika

Rinse peas well and place in large saucepan with enough fresh water to cover.
Bring to a boil and lower heat to a simmer. Cook until soft, replenishing the
liquid with boiling water as necessary. Drain and press cooked peas through
a sieve or puree in blender. Slowly add taheeni and lemon juice to the
chickpea puree. Add garlic and salt. Ingredients should make a thick,
smooth paste. If necessary, add water to thin. Pour into a shallow bowl.
Make a small hallow in the center and fill with olive oil. Garnish with parsley
and paprika. Chill. Serve as a dip with Arabic bread.

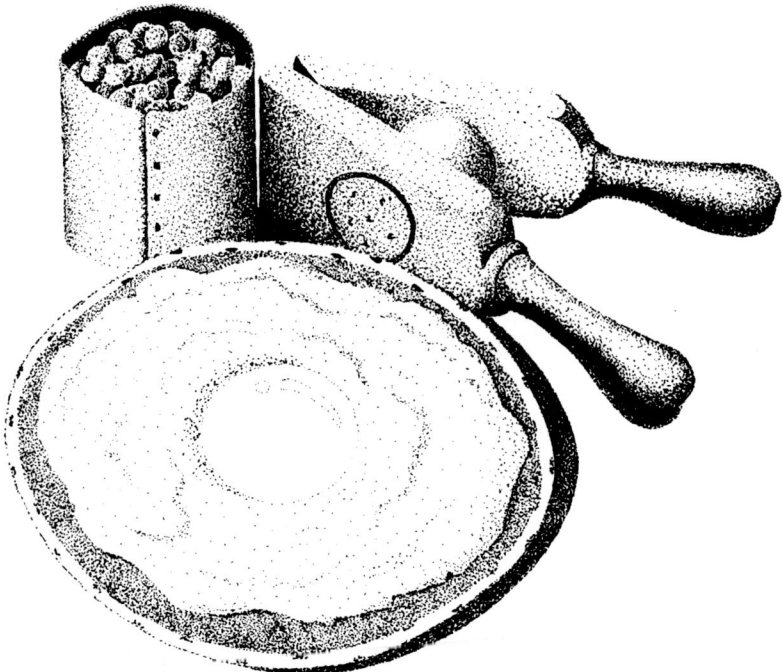

BAKLAVA

(LAYERED PASTRY WITH NUTS AND SYRUP)

350 grams butter, cut into 1/4 inch bits
6 tbls. vegetable oil
40 sheets phyllo pastry, defrosted
2 cups crushed walnuts

Melt butter slowly over a low heat, skim off the foam as it rises to the surface. Remove pan from heat, let it settle for 2 to 3 minutes, then spoon off the clear butter and discard the solids.

Preheat oven to 180°C (350° F). Combine the oil and clarified butter. Grease a 13x9x2 inch baking dish with about 12 grams of the butter mixture. Gently lift a sheet of phyllo into the greased dish. Flatten it against the bottom and fold the excess around the sides down. Brush the entire surface lightly with the butter mixture. Add another sheet of phyllo in the same way and sprinkle evenly with 2 1/2 tbls. of walnuts. Repeat this procedure of 2 sheets phyllo and 2 1/2 tbls. of walnuts to make 19 layers. Top off with the last 2 sheets of phyllo and brush with the remaining butter mixture. Score the top of the pastry with a knife, making parallel diagonal lines about 1/2 inch deep and 2 inches apart, then cross them diagonally to make diamond shapes. Bake in the center of the oven for 30 minutes. Reduce heat to 150°C (300° F) and bake for about 45 minutes longer, until top is crisp and golden.

Syrup:
1 1/2 cups sugar
2 1/2 tsps. fresh lemon juice
1/2 cups water
2 1/2 tsps. honey

While the baklava is baking, make the syrup. In a saucepan combine sugar, water and lemon juice, cook over a moderate heat until the sugar dissolves, stirring constantly. Increase the heat and, timing it from the moment the syrup boils, cook briskly, uncovered, for about 5 minutes. Remove from heat and stir in the honey. Pour into a bowl and refrigerate. When the baklava is done, remove it and pour the syrup over it. Cool to room temperature and cut into diamond shaped serving pieces.

MAMOOL

(ARAB COOKIES)

1 cup (230 grams) softened butter
2 cups flour
1/2 cup quick-cooking farina
1/4 tsp. ground nutmeg
dash ground cloves
2 tbls. water
1/4 tsp. orange water
1/4 cup finely chopped walnuts
1 tbls. granulated sugar
sifted powdered sugar

In large mixing bowl, cream butter until smooth. Stir together flour, farina and spices; add 1/2 to mixture, water and orange water. Mix well. Form dough into small balls (ping pong size). Hollow out the centers and fill with a mixture of the nuts and granulated sugar. Press dough back over filling. Press each cookie onto a buttered cookie sheet. Flatten and decorate with fork tines; or shape balls into wooden Arabic molds especially made for mamool before placing on the cookie sheet. Bake at 180°C (350° F) until lightly browned. Cool for 5 to 10 minutes and roll in powdered sugar. Yum Yum.

TAMR

(DATES WITH ALMONDS)

Dates (soft ripe fresh dates)
Almonds
Sesame seeds

Remove the date pits and mash the softened dates together. Use the 'tamr' — dates from the ripest stage as they are softer and more sugary. Heat the sesame seeds just till hot. Form the mashed dates into small balls with an almond in the center of each. Roll each ball in the sesame seeds and serve with Arab coffee. Delicious!

TALES FROM
ARABIA'S PAST

MOHAMMED THE PROPHET

In 570 AD a baby was born into a poor family of the Quraysh tribe in Makka, they called him Mohammed. Little did this Arab family realize what a monumental mark in history their son would make. Mohammed was orphaned at a young age and brought up by his grandfather and later by an uncle. Accompanying his Uncle Abu Talib on caravans, Mohammed learned the trade business and at the age of 25 he joined the caravan from Makka to Damascus in the employment of a wealthy widow, named Khadijah. The 40 year old widow soon proposed to Mohammed giving him new found wealth and position. They had six children but only four daughters survived.

During Mohammed's late thirties he began to retreat to the solitude of a desert cave where he would pray and meditate, escaping the pagan idolatry of Makka. It was during one of these moments that the archangel, Gabriel, first appeared to Mohammed instructing him to deliver Allah's word to all the Arab people. For over twenty years Mohammed received a series of revelations which he would in turn recite to someone close to him, who initially committed these revelations to memory but later recorded them in writing.

Initially Mohammed had self-doubt about his calling and preached these revelations only to his family and close friend Abu Bakr (Mohammed's father-in-law). Inspired by Khadijah's encouragement, Mohammed gained confidence that he had received a God-appointed task to devote himself to reforming religion and thus began extending his teachings to his tribe. Mohammed called all Makkans to believe in one God, Allah, the Merciful, but he found few converts. In fact, he was harassed and persecuted so much by the people of Makka that he made plans to flee the city. The Makkans were concerned that Mohammed's preaching of monotheism would deter the pilgrims from visiting the many shrines which brought in a major portion of the city's income. Mohammed fled the city in 622 with his family and followers to Yathrib, a city which was later called Medina (a shortened translation of 'City of the Prophet'). Mohammed's migration, or 'hijra,' to Yathrib marks the starting point of the Muslim calendar — this was Year 1. In Medina Mohammed was well received and the Islamic community grew with Islamic believers as he denounced idolatry and preached the surrender to the all powerful Allah, whose will is supreme and who determines man's fate.

Seven years later, in 630 AD, (Year 7 of the Islamic calendar), Mohammed marched on Makka with 10,000 faithful Islamic followers and conquered the city. Makka was now part of the ever growing Islamic community and was in fact established as the religious and political capital of Islam with the Kaaba set by Mohammed as the focal point of Islamic worship.

Mohammed never claimed to be more than mere mortal, but distinguished himself above others as Allah's chosen messenger and spokesman. He gave his people a great sense of pride and purpose within the Islamic society. Mohammed, the last of the great prophets, died in 632 AD in Medina, having begun the wheels of a great religious movement. "ALLAH IS GREAT. ALLAH IS ONE; AND MOHAMMED IS HIS MESSENGER."

JAHILIYYAH
This was the term used to describe the time before Mohammed and Islam, days of religious ignorance, days before the belief of only one God. This is a period in time of violence, polytheism and is unimportant to the Muslim Arab as far as Islam is concerned.

ZAM ZAM

Centuries ago, nearly 2000 years before the birth of Mohammed, Ibrahim, another prophet, was commanded by the Almighty God to abandon Hajjar, his wife, and their son, Ishmael, in the desolate desert. This was one of many tests God imposed upon Ibrahim as he committed his wife and son into His protection. Alone and desperate, Hajjar began searching for water for herself and her son in the barren valley between Mount Safa and Mount Marwa (the Western region of the Arabian peninsula). After searching between the mountain seven times she abandoned her search, and dropped to her knees to plead with Allah to help her and her son. Ishmael was crying and kicking his feet in the sand beside his mother. As his feet pushed at the sand, up came the water from a spring, the waters of Zam Zam! Her prayers had been answered. Bedouins wandering within the desert came upon Hajjar, Ishmael and their newly found water and asked for permission to settle in the valley. Soon Ibrahim returned to the valley to find Hajjar and Ishmael, and he labored to dig the well deeper

71

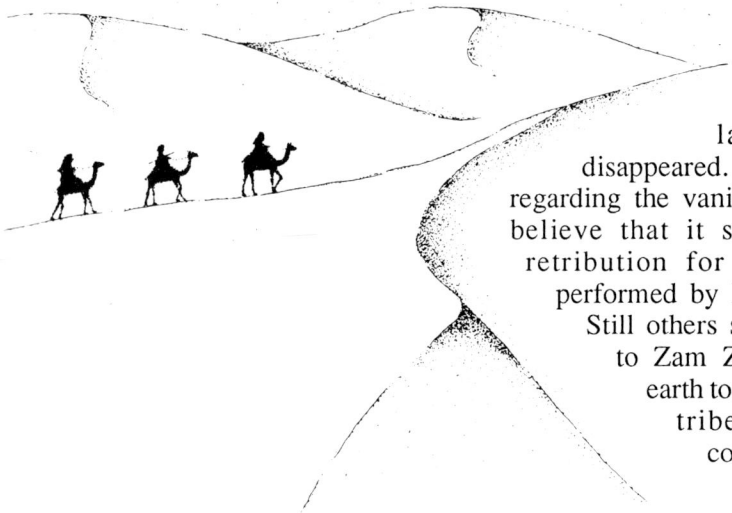

and reinforced it with a wall.

But many years later Zam Zam disappeared. Two stories are told regarding the vanishing spring. Some believe that it simply dried up in retribution for the pagan rituals performed by Makka's inhabitants. Still others say that the entrance to Zam Zam was filled with earth to hide it from attacking tribes and remained concealed for centuries. Zam Zam was not lost however, for Abdul Muttalib received a vision in a dream to dig for Zam Zam.

"What is Zam Zam?" Abdul Muttalib asked.

The voice in his dream answered, telling him of waters that would never run dry, about a spring that would offer water to the pilgrims of Makka.

When he awoke Abdul Muttalib went in search of Zam Zam, following the signs of his vision. His search took him into a sanctuary not far from the Holy Kaaba. Despite opposition and astonishment from his friends Abdul Muttalib set about digging for Zam Zam near this sanctuary. For days he dug and dug until the waters of the spring bubbled up from the earth once again! He became guardian of the well and provided full basins of drawn water for the pilgrims. During these early days the water was salty so Abdul Muttalib would sweeten it with dates or raisins, or with honey and camel's milk.

To this day the faithful have been drinking the waters of the seemingly inexhaustible Zam Zam in Makka, which are considered to be blessed by Allah and therefore able to cure the ill. Believers say that when they drink these miraculous waters they may acquire wisdom and faith. Still others recite a supplication to Allah while drinking the water and ask for personal assistance. They also say it relieves stomach aches. Many even take a sealed clay container, or plastic one nowadays, with them upon leaving the Great Haram, the mosque where the waters flow. The residents of Makka depend upon the Zam Zam spring as their main water supply and are thus privileged to drink the waters year round.

During the 20th century the amount of pilgrims arriving in Makka has increased tremendously. In 1945 King Abdul Aziz Ibn Saud issued a Royal decree to expand the Great Haram, the sacred mosque of Makka and to modernize Zam Zam's facilities. In 1976 the Zam Zam area was completely reconstructed to serve more worshippers and to keep the water safe and clear. A refrigeration unit has even been added to keep the waters ever cool. From waters once bubbling freely to the sand's surface, Zam Zam is now a marble-lined underground area with over 300 faucets throughout the mosque. The sacred water of Zam Zam will continue to quench the thirst of the millions of believers who pilgrimage to Makka every year.

1001 ARABIAN NIGHTS

The Arabian Nights is a collection of 8th to 16th century folkloric stories originating in Arabia, India and Persia. The collection is based around a frame story of Persian origin about a woman named Scheherazade who is sentenced to die at dawn by her husband, King Schahriah. Clever Scheherazade saves her life by beguiling her husband with a series of night-long tales for 1001 nights by saving the ending of each story until the next night. Three of the most famous stories include "Aladdin's Lamp," "Sinbad the Sailor," and "Ali Baba and the Forty Thieves."

LAWRENCE OF ARABIA

When we speak of Arabia the legendary name of 'Lawrence of Arabia' comes to mind — a man immortalized as a handsome hero of Arabia through the glitter and glamour of Hollywood.

As a British soldier, T.E. Lawrence (1888-1935) went to Arabia during WWI when the west was showing an interest in the strategic position of the Arabs. After inspecting the Arab-Turk situation in the Hejaz region along the Red Sea coast Lawrence suggested to his superiors that British armed forces would not resolve the problem but instead offered himself as adviser to the Arabs. So Lawrence teamed up with Shareef Husain, the leader of the Hashimite forces, to rid the area of the Turks. T.E. Lawrence and the Hashimite forces captured the city of Aqaba on the Red Sea north of Medina. Their successful guerrilla campaign was to interrupt the Turks supply lines by blowing up the Hejaz railway lines that ran the supplies down from Damascus to Medina. He was also with the forces that captured Damascus in 1918.

As an English scholar and writer T.E. Lawrence gives a detailed account of his Arabian campaign in his book entitled "The Seven Pillars of Wisdom."

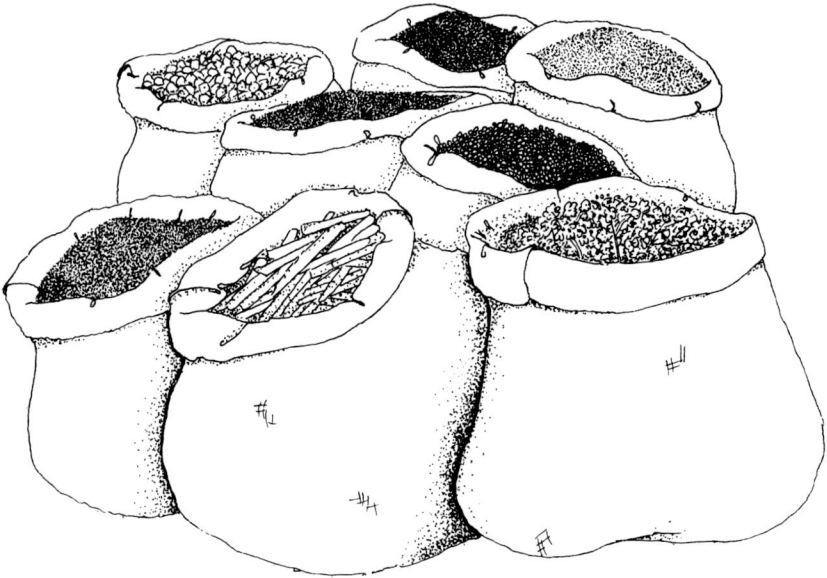

FRANKINCENSE AND MYRRH

"They Presented Unto Him Gifts: Gold, Frankincense and Myrrh. By gold was shown the power of a King, for gold pertaineth to tribute; by incense was shown divine majesty, for incense pertaineth to sacrifice; by myrrh was shown man's mortality, for myrrh pertaineth to burial."

Centuries before oil was discovered under the desert sands and long before the age of Islam the Arabian peninsula was called Arabia Felix (Happy Arabia), contented by the wealth from the frankincense trade. From the southern tip, in the Dhofar region of Oman, the trade route began its long journey, first via ship to the port of Qana in Yemen and then overland travelling northward through Arabia Felix by camel caravans. The wealth brought by the trade was dependent upon the existence of the camel, the one animal that is uniquely adaptable to the harsh desert and is able to carry large loads.

Along the route of the camel caravan, Arabian cities, such as Medina and Makka, grew and prospered. Merchants in these cities traded their prized frankincense for silks, spices and gold from the Orient. It was also in high demand by the Greeks and Romans who used it during pagan rituals. Frankincense was used lavishly during cremations to mask the pungent odor of the burning body. Along with frankincense, myrrh, which was three times the price, was traded along the incense route. Both were symbols of great wealth. Besides the use as a fumigant other traditional uses of frankincense and myrrh included cooking, as a perfume additive, embalming and medicinal purposes.

Frankincense, an aromatic gum resin native to Ethiopia and the southern Arabian peninsula comes from the harvesting of small trees of the genus Boswellia. From scores cut into the bark a milk-white resin oozes like sap from the wounds. As the resin hardens it changes to a lucid amber color. Myrrh is darker in color and said to be richer in fragrance. Harvesting of the resin, which is broken up for use, goes on nearly all year round.

What happened to the demand for frankincense and myrrh and thus the wealth it brought? First of all the rise of Christianity started their downfall as it brought a stop to pagan rituals, thus the lack of need for frankincense and myrrh. The rise of Islam after 622 AD further reduced the frankincense trade as Islamic rituals rarely require incense. Also, as wealth from trade came to the people of Arabia they were able to afford the more expensive incenses, such as sandalwood.

Today only a few tons of frankincense are produced each year with the principle harvesting area for the finest being the Dhofar region of Oman. As the Arabs burn frankincense on hot charcoals fanning the smoke into their clothes and hair, the camel caravans continue to carry a variety of goods along the centuries old incense route.

PERFUMES OF ARABIA

"If you stand near a blacksmith you will get covered in soot, but if you stand near a perfume seller you will carry an aroma of scent with you." From the HADITH

Along with the treasured incense, aromatic attar was carried along the legendary camel caravan routes. A gift of perfumed oil from Arabia was a high compliment to pay to any one, along with the welcome of burning incense. These sweet scents are enhanced by the beautiful bottles craftsmen design to store the attar. One of the most prized scents is the attar of roses simply made from crushed rose petals. Other scents include jasmine, lavender, even henna, a robust scent used as a perfume long before the plant was known to produce a beautiful dye. The tradition of these scents will continue for time immemorial.

A DOMAIN OF KINGS

Arabian history has been passed from one generation to the next in the tradition of poetry and story telling. The expressive beauty of the Arabic language has preserved the tales of history in a sense of honor and splendor. This tale begins in the 7th century with the coming of Islam which served to unify the Semitic nomad tribes. Mohammed's Islamic followers, led by the caliphs, founded a great empire that grew as the centuries passed. Arab conquests were made that extended from Spain to India. During the 16th century the Turks established a rule over much of Arabia and during the 18th century Arabia began dividing into separate tribal principalities.

It is here that the great King Ibn Saud joins our story for it is he who almost entirely created the Kingdom of Saudi Arabia. Since the 1700's the House of Saud had ruled the central region of Arabia with Diriyyah, a city north of Riyadh, being their capital seat. By the late 1800's the rule of the Saud tribe fell to the Rashids, a rival family. The head of the Saud household fled in exile to Kuwait with his children in his saddle bags - one was Ibn Saud. Ibn Saud grew up in Kuwait and at the age of 21, in 1901, he returned to Arabia and attacked Riyadh with 40 able men on camelback. He had regained the former glory of the House of Saud. Under the Islamic

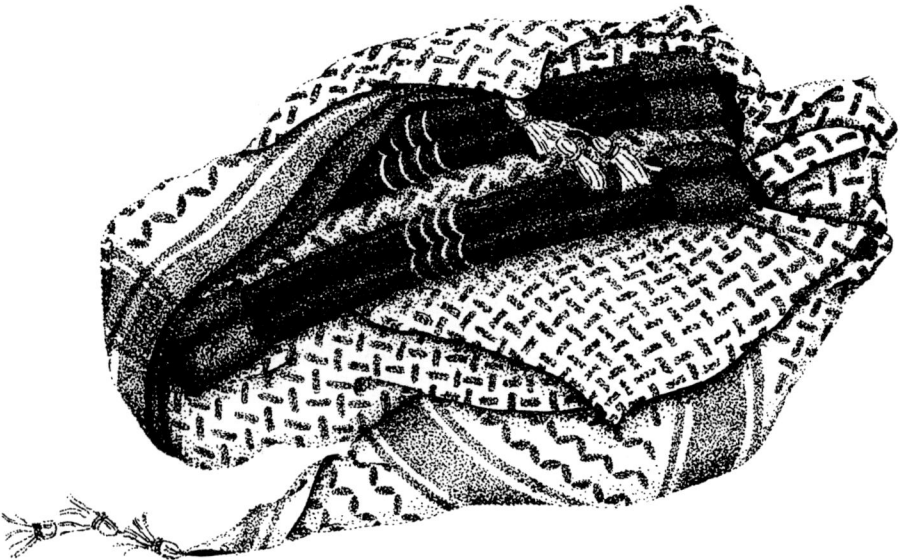

banner Ibn Saud assembled his followers and began uniting the tribes of Arabia, who were drawn to his return to the basic principles of Islam. Ibn Saud fought many victorious battles against his rivals taking rule over region by region, generously adopting children of slain leaders and marrying wives from other tribes to expand his rule. By 1932 Ibn Saud had carved his empire, which was named the Kingdom of Saudi Arabia after the Saud family!

On the day of King Ibn Saud's death in 1953 his sons began the succession of royal lineage. It is reported that he had over 40 sons, although the daughters were never counted. His eldest son, Saud, reigned for 11 years. In 1964 Kind Saud was deposed due to his ailing health and was succeeded by Crown Prince Faisal. After 11 years of successfully improving his desert Kingdom King Faisal was assassinated by a deranged kinsman. Although the event shook the Middle East it did not alter Saudi Arabia's course as his brother Prince Khalid smoothly took over the reign. In 1982 King Khalid died of a heart attack and his half-brother, Prince Fahd bin Abdul Aziz became the new king with his half-brother Abdulla chosen as Crown prince.

Although this country of mysterious legend has been inhabited for thousands of years it has been a unified nation ruled by Kings since only 1932.

OIL! OIL!

Black gold was discovered in the 1920's in Bahrain, the tiny island off the coast of Saudi Arabia in the Persian Gulf, or Arabian Gulf as it is referred to by the Saudis. A New Zealander by the name of Major Frank Holmes pursued the possibility that these oil reserves were even greater beneath the massive mainland of Saudi Arabia and so went to Arabia to negotiate with King Abdul Aziz, the new ruler of that giant peninsula. Although Major Holmes was successful in obtaining a concession in the eastern province to search for oil, the concession lapsed for the lack of funds and they discontinued their search. In 1933, only half a century ago, American geologists approached the King, again asking his permission to drill into his arid land, assuring him that they would pay him highly. King Abdul Aziz did give the foreign geologists the 'go ahead' to drill, however, he was hoping they would find a different wealth beneath those sands. He was hoping for water, water for the dry desert, water for his people, this would be a great wealth for a desert King to have!

You can imagine the initial disappointment felt by the King and his desert people when a black gooey substance came out of the ground instead of water for Saudi Arabia was far from being an industrialized country and but for a handful of cars had no need for this black oil.

Well #7 in Dammam was the first to turn Arabia's fortunes. World War II slowed the oil boom down, restricting its development slightly as danger of transporting oil across the war ridden seas was eminent. But by the war's end, the fall of 1943 showed continued development, and soon the full potential was realized and large scale production was set in motion. An impressive change in wealth occurred in the Kingdom of Saudi Arabia, and centuries-old ways of life began to alter. Under ibn Saud's rule, before the coming of oil, Saudi's entire treasury was kept in a tin box. Now, virtually without warning Saudi Arabia underwent the fastest modernization experienced by any country, lifting these quiet nomads from their simple lives into the fast pace twentieth century. As time went by more and more oil fields were discovered, more roads were built and cities grew larger. It is believed that Saudi Arabia holds a quarter of the known oil reserves of the world.

The oil dollars are shared with all the Kingdom's people. Every Saudi male may go to the government at the age of 18 and ask for a sum of money to build his own home, to be paid back in 25 years interest free, (usury is forbidden according to Islamic beliefs). He may also ask for money for a business or for marriage under the same terms. The oil discovery has not only brought wealth to the pockets of its people, but it has improved the living standards of its people by providing free education, free medical care, universities, sophisticated hospitals and a tax-free state.

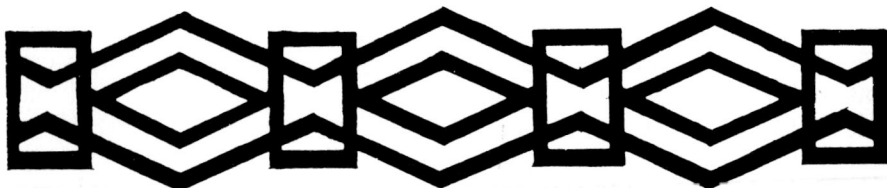

UNDERSTANDING ISLAM

ISLAM

"There is no God but Allah, and Mohammed is His messenger." This creed (shahaada) essentially sums up the beliefs of Islam, a major religion with its roots profoundly established amongst the peoples of the Arabian peninsula and extending from Northern Africa to Indonesia. The Arabic word 'Islam' means "submission to God," and the God in whom the Islamic faithful believe in, is a single entity. Allah, simply the Arabic word for "God," of Islam is the creator of the universe and the force for good in all things, a concept that is not too dissimilar from the beliefs of Christian religions.

The Quran, the Muslims' holy book, is considered to be the very word of God, revealed to Mohammed by the angel Gabriel. It lays down all the fundamental laws of Islam, and a thorough knowledge of it is traditionally considered to be a corner stone of every Muslim's education. Muslims have five duties to follow, called the "Pillars of the Faith," and are really the basis of Islam — the Shahaada (recitation of the creed), the Salaat (prayer five times daily while facing Makka), the Zakat (alms giving), the Siam (fasting during Ramadan), and the Hajj (pilgrimage to Makka).

In addition to the five pillars of the faith, Islamic law dictates the following — Muslims may not drink alcoholic beverages, Muslims may not eat pork, Muslims may not gamble, Muslim men may have up to four wives as long as they can treat them all equally in every way, and Muslims may eat only the flesh of properly slaughtered animals, and may not eat flesh in which the blood is visible. Islam is the basis for life in Saudi Arabia, for culture, customs and for social well being.

DID YOU KNOW THAT . . .

The Muslims recognize Jesus as a great prophet before Mohammed, the last and greatest of all prophets. They also believe in the Virgin Mary, but they do not believe Jesus was the son of God nor do they believe in Jesus' resurrection. Muslims believe both Mohammed and Jesus to have been ordinary men, with God appointed tasks.

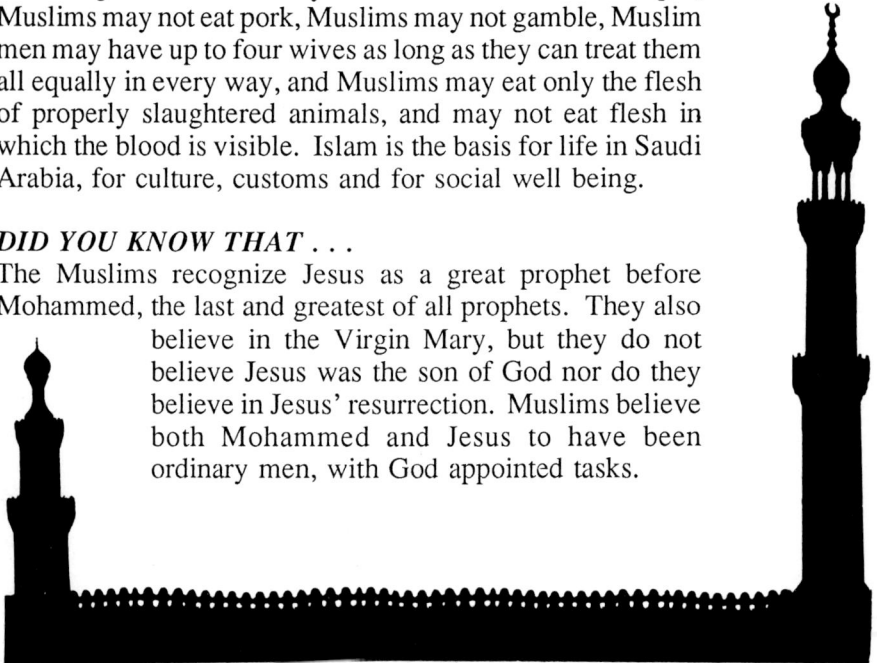

80

SUNNITES AND SHI'AITES

After Mohammed's death, the Muslims became divided into two groups, the Sunnites and the Shi'aites. Sunnies are Muslims of the Sunnah community and are a majority amongst the Muslims, strictly following the Sunnah practices of the Prophet Mohammed. The term 'sunnah' is derived from the traditional 'way' or 'sunnah' of the Prophet.

The Shi'as, the other major Islamic branch, derive their name from the Arabic 'shi'at Ali' or 'the party of Ali.' The Shi'aites reject the first three caliphs that succeeded after Mohammed's death and recognize Mohammed's son-in-law, Ali, (of Mohammed and Khadijah's children, only daughters survived) and his descendents as the rightful successors of Mohammed.

DID YOU KNOW THAT . . .
Following the death of the Prophet Mohammed in 632 Abu Bakr was chosen as the first Muslim caliph of Arabia. Abu Bakr was the Prophet's father-in-law and one of his earliest followers.

ଠଠଠଠଠଠ ଠଠ ଠଠଠଠଠଠଠଠଠଠଠଠଠଠଠଠଠଠଠଠଠଠଠଠଠଠ

IMPURITY

According to Islamic beliefs certain animals or substances are considered impure. Dead animals are considered impure except for those slaughtered in the proper Islamic way. An animal that is killed for human consumption, Muslim consumption, must be slaughtered by cutting the throat and saying "Bismallah, Allah Akbar." (In the name of God, God is most Great.) This strictness regarding impurity also applies to any limb or organ cut off from any living animal before being slaughtered. However, there are a few exceptions according to the Prophet Mohammed. "Two kinds of dead animals and two types of blood are made lawful to us. The dead are fish and locusts and the bloods are the liver and the spleen." Other dead animals, such as ants or bees are also an exception to the Islam's impurity beliefs, to the extent that if they fall into a liquid and die, the liquid remains pure, unless the liquid is changed.

Bones, hair, nails, horns, feathers and skin of any dead animal are some other impurity exceptions as there is no evidence to suggest that they are impure, according to Islam. Therefore, only what could be eaten is considered impure when an animal dies naturally.

Blood pouring from an animal, even a slaughtered one, is impure. The traces of blood that remain in the veins are permissible to consume.

Pus, however is not impure but should be washed away with water.

Swine meat is undoubtedly considered impure according to the Quran. Therefore pork is not available in any form in the local supermarkets. In fact, even if a suggested recipe on a food product container calls for pork, the word will be blackened out. The Prophet Mohammed denounced this meat in the 7th century AD. The Quran says: "Forbidden to you are carrion, blood, the flesh of swine, what has been hallowed to other than God, the beast strangled . . . "

DID YOU KNOW THAT . . .
Muslims consider dogs impure. When a dog drinks from a dish it must be washed seven times, the first of which should be a mixture of water and sand. However, dog's hair is considered to be pure.

THE HOLY QURAN

The oldest Arabic book and sacred scripture of the Islamic religion is the Holy Quran. Muslims regard the Quran as God's actual eternal words revealed to Mohammed in the 7th century. The angel Gabriel appeared before Mohammed and revealed to him that he should preach the word of one God, Allah. At that time polytheism was the flavor of the day. For over 20 years Mohammed received messages of Allah's words through the angel. Shortly after each divine message was revealed to Mohammed he would recite it to someone who soon wrote it down on whatever was available, palm leaves, stones, even leather. Mohammed, God's messenger, passed on the Word of Allah and over many years a large Islamic following grew. After his death the collection of verses were compiled together by the Caliphs into one book, the Quran, and to this day these words remain the Word of God.

Comprised of laws, fundamental moral instructions and recitations, the Quran is divided into 114 'suras' or chapters, arranged according to length from the longest to the shortest except for the brief opening prayer. Stressing Allah's compassion and mercy the Quran demands total surrender to the Will of Allah. The name 'Quran' originates from the Arabic root word 'karaa' (to read) and means reading aloud or chanting. Additional Islamic reading is found in the Hadith (tradition), a collection of sayings and teachings of the Prophet Mohammed that Muslims reflect upon for life's social and moral actions. The Quran not only prescribes religious directives but also decrees the guidelines for social life, family life, criminal laws and inheritance laws, for example — in other words the complete basis for Muslim life!

The words of God in the Quran influence everyday life and portions represent the basis for the midday sermons given every Friday, Islamic holy day (compared to our Sunday). The traditional Arabic used in the Quran is universal throughout the entire Muslim world from Morocco in the West to Indonesia in the East. Quranic verse may often be referred to in ordinary conversation and links Muslims everywhere.

DID YOU KNOW THAT . . .
It is considered extremely improper and disrespectful to place books or other objects on top of the Holy Quran.

ISLAMIC LAW

"EYE FOR AN EYE AND TOOTH FOR A TOOTH."

The Sharia'a or Islamic law, based on the revelations received by the Prophet Mohammed, is a complex system that includes the Bedouin's perception of justice of 'an eye for an eye.' Religion is the State and the State is religion, they are one. The Quran indicates the crimes against society and Islam, and then defines the punishments. A thief, for example, after several overt offenses will have his right hand severed. This offender is dealt a double blow for now not only is he missing a hand but he must eat in private as he must use his left hand, an Islamic taboo. Public floggings are given for a variety of crimes, even today in the 20th century. There are three crimes that carry the death penalty: denial of Islamic faith, homicide, and adultery. Capital punishment is usually death by decapitation unless unusual circumstances dictate a life sentence. Another method of capital punishment is stoning, also continued into this century. Punishments are carried out in public to set an example, deterring other possible offenders. These punishments may appear harsh to Westerners, but beheading is swift and more humane than most methods. Justice is harsh. As a foreigner you may be shocked by such methods, but no more than the Arab is shocked by our high crime rates in the west. The crime rate of Saudi Arabia, the heart of Islam is said to be one of the lowest in the world.

PRAYER

Five times a day the muezzin, trained in chanting skills, calls the faithful from the mosque to come pray. The calls are commonly made from a loudspeaker just before sunrise (fajr), midday (dohr), late afternoon (aser), sunset (maghrib), and nightfall (esha). The compelling call announces prayer time, whereby Muslims go to the nearest mosque to pray or pray at their home or job site. It is not uncommon to see an Arab praying alongside the freeway upon his prayer matt, if that is where he is when prayer time commences. Devotion to daily prayer is one of the five pillars of Islamic faith.

Prayer announcements from mosques all over town overflow into each other, for it is said that a man's place of prayer should be no more than five minutes walk from his home.

"Allah Akbar!
Allah Akbar!
Allah Akbar!
Allah Akbar! .... (God is most great.)
Ashad an la ilah illa Allah!
Ashad an la ilah illa Allah!
.... (I witness no God but Allah.)
Ashad an Mohammed rasoul Allah!
Ashad an Mohammed rasoul Allah!
.. (I witness Mohammed, the messenger of Allah.)
Hai ala alsalah!
Hai ala alsalah! .... (Come to prayer.)
Hai ala alfalah!
Hai ala alfalah! .... (Come for prosperity.)
Allah akbar!
Allah akbar! .... (God is most great.)
La ilah illa Allah!" .... (No God but Allah.)

Thus the summons goes five times daily delivered over loudspeaker from every mosque in the world. In some small villages there are no loudspeakers at the mosques and just like in the days of old, the muezzin announces prayer time from the heights of the minaret.

84

Before prayer each Muslim performs ablution, the cleansing ritual — washing of the face, hands, arms to the elbows and feet to the ankles. This cleansing symbolically washes away sin before coming to God in prayer. During prayer Muslims face in the direction of the Holy Kaaba in Makka. There are no priests as such at the mosque, instead worship is led by an 'imam,' a non-cleric leader, studied in the Quran. Islamic prayer is essentially an individual's personal bonding to God.

THE FIVE PILLARS OF FAITH

Muslims, men and women, have accepted five duties as part of their Islamic faith. Each duty is described in the Holy Quran.

• The first pillar is profession of faith. This faithful declaration of this creed is to be repeated, "there is no God but Allah and Mohammed is the Messenger of God."

• The second pillar is devotion to prayer. Prayer is to be performed five times daily — just before sunrise, midday, late afternoon, sunset and nightfall — while facing the Holy Kaaba in Makka. Wherever a Muslim is during prayer time he performs his prayer ritual individually or with other devout. On Fridays a midday congregational is performed at the al-Juma, or Friday Mosque, prior to a lengthy sermon.

• The third pillar is alms giving, or 'zakat.' Muslims are obliged to pay a religious tax to their government for charitable works. Muslims also have a responsibility to donate gifts personally to the needy. This duty helps the entire Muslim community.

• The fourth pillar is fasting during Ramadan. It is written in the Quran that during the ninth month of the Islamic calendar Muslims must observe complete abstinence from food and drink during daylight hours.

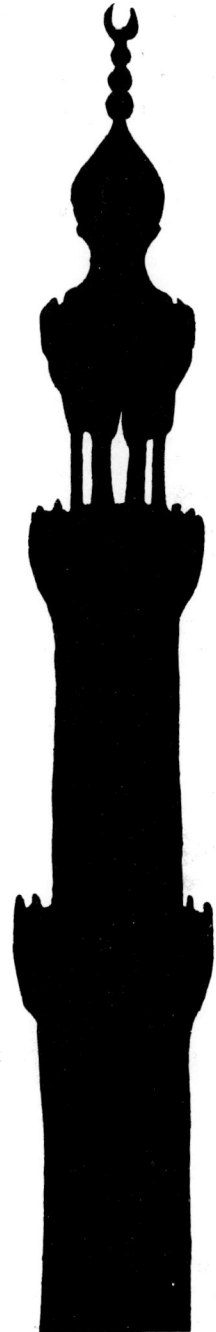

•   The fifth pillar is a pilgramage (hajj) to Makka. The duty required of those Muslims who can afford it is to make a pilgrimage to Makka. The hajj should be completed on the 8th, 9th, and 10th days of Dhu al Hijjah, the 12th month. Muslims from all over the world migrate to Makka annually during this time. A lesser pilgrimage, 'umrah,' can be done any time of the year and incorporates most of the rituals of hajj.

☿☿☿☿☿☿ ☿☿ ☿☿☿☿☿☿☿☿☿☿☿☿☿☿☿☿☿☿☿☿☿☿☿☿☿☿☿

THE HOLY KAABA

The Kaaba stands in the center of a vast courtyard of marble within the Great Mosque of Makka. This shrine is the geographical and spiritual center of Islam, to which all Muslims face five times a day during prayer.

Pilgrims to Makka must circle the flat-roofed Kaaba seven times, sick and old are carried aloft on litters. At its eastern corner there is the Black Stone, that was kissed by the Prophet Mohammed. The sacred Black Stone is set in a silver frame on a corner wall. The Kaaba, draped in a heavy black cloth embroidered with verses from the Quran, is a building of blocks standing 50 feet high and is hollow within. Called the House of God (Bait Allah), it is said that the great Biblical patriarch Ibrahim was commanded by God to build the Holy Kaaba. It has been rebuilt since Ibrahim's times. Before Mohammed's call to Islam Arabs worshipped many lesser gods. While Mohammed was in Medina he and the Muslim people would face toward Kutuz (Jerusalem) during prayer. After the revelations from Allah and when Mohammed returned to Makka the Muslims turned to face the Kaaba for prayer.

DID YOU KNOW THAT . . .
Vendors outside the Great Mosque in Makka sell prayer compasses that point toward Makka from any spot on earth — a useful item for world travellers.

☿☿☿☿☿☿ ☿☿ ☿☿☿☿☿☿☿☿☿☿☿☿☿☿☿☿☿☿☿☿☿☿☿☿☿☿☿

MOSQUES

There are two indispensable characteristics of Muslim life seen in every town, the market place and the Friday mosque. The mosque is the Muslims' house of worship, a place where Muslims of all walks of life can gather and meet with one another. The name 'mosque' originates from the

Arabic word 'masjid' meaning "a place for prostration" (during prayer).

Muslims shed their shoes before entering any mosque. Public worship takes place daily at the mosque. There are three different kinds of mosques — the small neighborhood mosque that is within five minutes walking distance of the devout; the larger al-juma (Friday) mosque that can hold 4000 to 5000 prayers when special Friday sermons are given at midday; and the third type is the Eid mosque which is generally an open

air fenced-in area with room for 400,000 prayers during the Eid holidays.

The beauty of the mosque is seen in the variety of elaborate designs built throughout the Islamic world, however there are certain features found at most mosques. These features include the courtyard or 'sahn,' which has a water fountain for ablution, for the ritual cleansing before prayer; the sanctuary or sheltered area for prayer that has a 'mihrah,' a recess in the wall that denotes the direction of Makka and thus the direction to face while praying; the 'mimbar,' a raised platform for the Imam (the assemblage prayer leader); and the minaret from where the muezzin calls the faithful to prayers.

The Prophet Mohammed denounced idolatry and thus to this day mosques do not contain forbidden relics or images of God. They are, however decorated with symmetrical abstract patterns, an art form common throughout the Middle East.

DID YOU KNOW THAT . . .
Quran verses are used to treat ailments. A chapter from the Quran is written on a plate and plain water or rosewater is poured on the plate dissolving the writing. This liquid is given to a patient to drink. Another method is when a patient relative of a patient stands at the door of the Mosque with a cup of water. Each member of the congregation breathes into the water as he comes out, some may even recite a verse or two from the Quran into the water. All of this is done to aid in the recovery of the patient who drinks the contents of the cup.

PRAYER BEADS

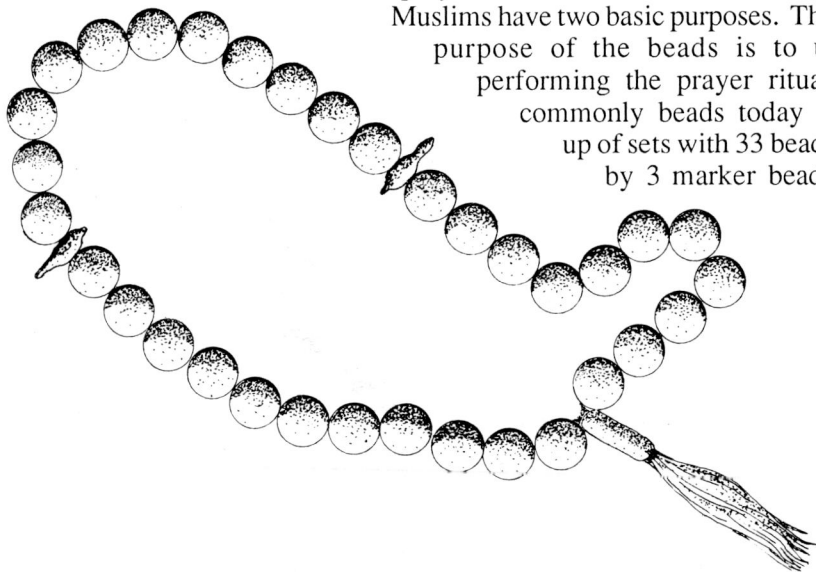

The prayer beads or 'misbaha' often seen held by Muslims have two basic purposes. The original purpose of the beads is to use after performing the prayer ritual. Most commonly beads today are made up of sets with 33 beads divided by 3 marker beads — one starter or indicator bead and two separator beads that divided them into three groups of 11 beads. The beads are used as counters 3 times around during an individual's final prayers. Three prayer statements are said 33 times —

"GLORY TO ALLAH
PRAISE TO ALLAH
ALLAH IS THE GREATEST"
A final statement, the 100th, is —
"NO GOD BUT ALLAH."

The secondary purpose is to keep the hands busy, thus the common term "worry" beads. Prayer beads range in price depending on what they are made from — plastic, wood, precious or semi-precious stones or metal such as silver or gold.

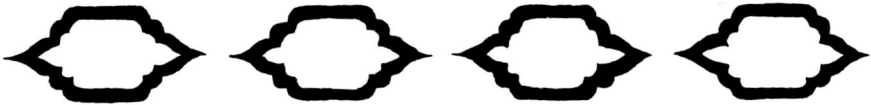

HAJJ

Al-Hajj is the duty of all Muslims, both men and women, to make a pilgrimage to Makka at least once in their lifetime if they have the physical or economical means to do so. As the largest single annual migration in the world, al-hajj represents a special moment in the faithfuls' lifetime of devotion to Allah.

The hajj takes place only once a year during the 8th, 9th, and 10th of Dhu al Hijjah, the 12th month of the Muslim calendar. There is a lesser pilgrimage or visit to Makka called 'umrah' which can be completed any time of the year. The umrah consists of several rituals, the first of which is to circle the Holy Kaaba. Pilgrims begin at the Black Stone and circle the Kaaba seven times in an anti-clockwise direction. Each time a pilgrim passes the Black Stone, embedded within a corner of the Kaaba, he either kisses or touches it if he is close enough, otherwise he will wave his hand toward the stone.

Al Haram, as the Great Mosque of Makka is called, with its soaring minarets, marble walls and exquisite Arab architecture, is an impressive sight to the visiting pilgrims. The twin minarets guard the entrance to Al Haram like sentries on duty. Continuing the pilgrimage ritual, the pilgrims leave the Great Mosque, embarking on the second part of the umrah ritual which entails running between the two hills of As Safa and Al Marwa. Pilgrims hasten between the hills seven times, all the time reciting prayers and supplications. The pilgrims end up at Al Marwa where the third and final part of this mini-hajj takes place — having the hair of their head cut or shaved.

At a designated point upon approaching the holy city of Makka each pilgrim enters into a state of purity known as 'ihram.' Before commencing the hajj rituals therefore, pilgrims do ablution and prayers. They also don sandals and two seamless cloths, one to wrap around the lower part of the body and the other to drape over the shoulder. Dressing the same and so simply expresses equality among all the pilgrims before God. Women wear white robes but have no special dress except that they must not cover their faces no matter what their customs may be.

The full hajj rituals, which are carefully prescribed, combine those of the umrah with additional rites outside of Makka. Some pilgrims use the services of professional pilgrimage guides, or 'mutawif.' During hajj the pilgrims congregate at the plain of Arafat, 12 miles southeast of Makka. This is where the Prophet gave his farewell sermon in which he summarized the duties of a Muslim. The time here is spent making friends, reciting dissertations and prayers. This once barren valley becomes a sea of tents during the annual hajj. At sunset a cannon shot signals the pilgrims to proceed to Mina, five miles away. Each pilgrim gathers 7 small stones along the way. The stones are hurled at one of three white pillars in Mina, the one closest to Makka. This symbolic ritual enacts the ceremony called "stoning the devil." As they toss their stones the pilgrims call out "Allah Akbar, Allah Akbar," — God is Great. The pillars commemorate the place where Ibrahim was tempted by the devil as he was about to sacrifice his son to God. The devil appeared before Ibrahim three times. As the pilgrims throw their stones they are showing their own resistance to temptation. As Ibrahim was about to sacrifice his son, God replaced his son with a ram. This symbolic sacrifice has survived to this day, as thousands of sheep and small numbers of cattle and camels are slaughtered either by the pilgrims or in special

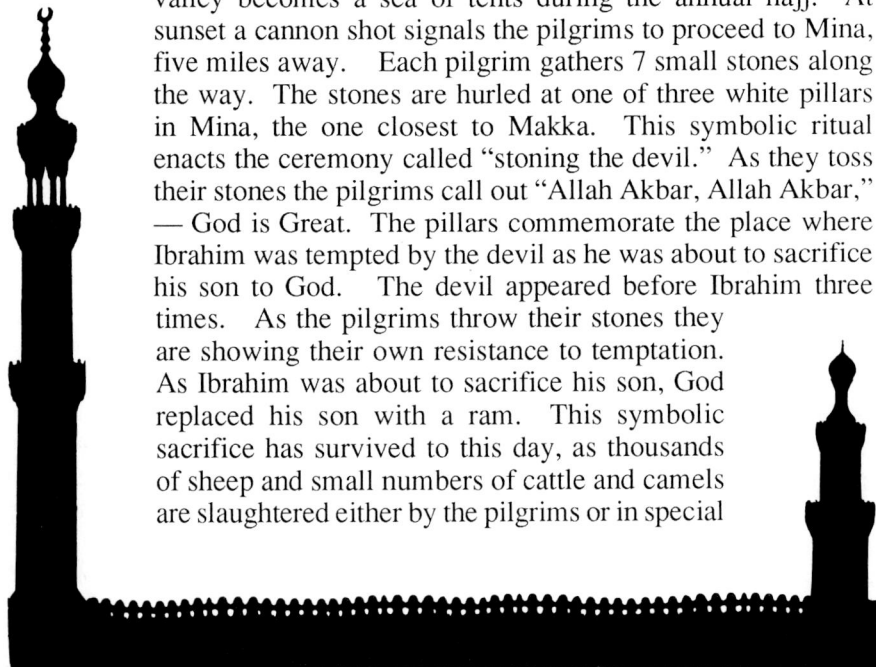

slaughter houses during the final day of hajj. Each pilgrim keeps a cut of the meat and distributes the rest to the poor and needy.

The pilgrims then return to Makka to circle the Kaaba and to run in the valley between the two hills. Upon having their hair and nails cut their hajj is completed. Each pilgrim washes and dresses in new clothes to return home.

Due to easy access to Makka with today's modern air and sea travel hundreds of thousands of pilgrims from all over the world visit Makka each year. Saudi Arabia puts forth great efforts to make the visit a peaceful and memorable one. Some of the ways this host country helps out include improved road systems, improved airport facilities, additional accommodation along with many other security, commercial or cultural services. When hajj occurs during the hot summer months the Ministry of Health provides sunstroke treatment facilities and there are a large number of air-conditioned medical buildings to aid the pilgrims. Saudi Arabia will continue to provide for the coming pilgrims as the numbers are sure to increase in the years to come.

THE HOLY MONTH OF RAMADAN

Ramadan, the ninth month of the Muslim calendar, was the time of the year when the Prophet Mohammed first received God's revelations. Annually a period of obligatory fasting commemorates the revelation of the Quran. Throughout the month Muslims must abstain from eating, drinking, smoking, and other bodily pleasures during daylight hours. The fast also includes no submersion in water and no medicines. Persons who are sick, pregnant women, young children, and travellers are exempt from fasting during Ramadan. However, any missed days must be made up at the earliest opportunity before the next Ramadan. Children begin observing Ramadan around the age of 12 or puberty. This monthly fast is the severest of trials, a test of discipline, especially when Ramadan falls during the hot summer season (the Muslim lunar calendar revolves through the solar year).

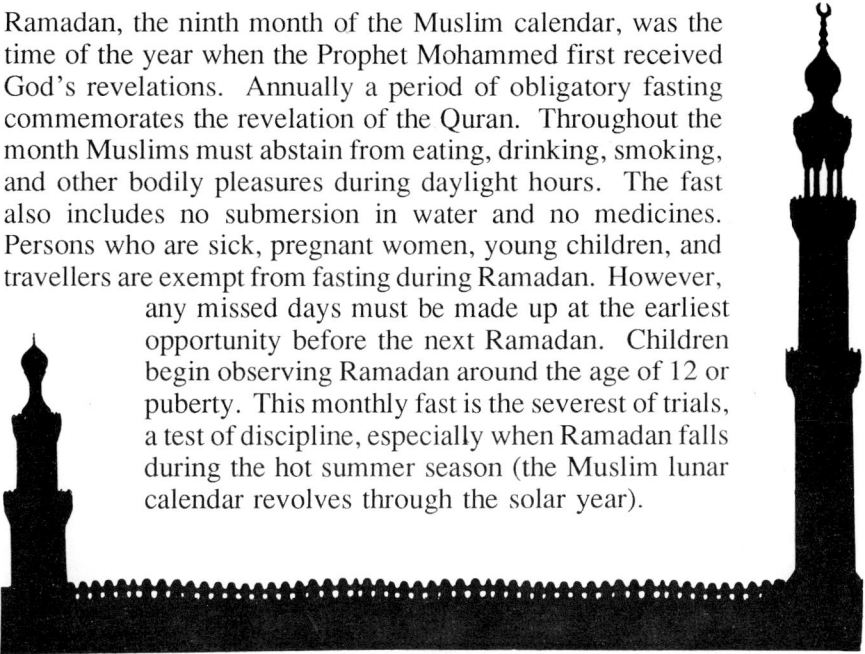

91

In the month of Ramadan, Muslims are attempting to achieve 'humility,' 'equality,' 'self-control,' 'patience,' 'physical good health,' 'community,' and 'generosity.'

Although the fasting may seem to be a time of hardship and suffering, it is more a time of rejoicing, rejoicing the wisdom of Allah and the Prophethood of Mohammed. For when the sun goes down and a cannon shot is fired a meal will break the daily fast and will initiate a night of feasting, family gatherings, celebration, and prayer. Before sunrise and the morning cannon shot signalling the start of a new day of fasting a large meal is prepared and served. Centuries ago in small isolated villages and Bedouin camps, sunrise and sunset was decided by being able to distinguish two threads — one black and one white. "And eat and drink, until the white thread of dawn appears distinct from its black thread." — (Surat al-Bagarah, verse no. 196 in the Quran).

During Ramadan daytime and nighttime activities are virtually reversed, naps during the day help make up for the lack of evening sleep. Stores may open for a short period in the morning but do not open again until 8 p.m. or 9 p.m., often staying open very late. Workers may work shorter hours, usually only six instead of the regular eight.

Although non-Muslims do not have to fast, as a gesture of respect and understanding, they should not eat, drink, or smoke in public during the daylight hours of Ramadan.

For three days after Ramadan, during the month of Shawwal, Eid al-Fitr (The Feast of Breaking Fast) is celebrated.

DID YOU KNOW THAT . . .
Sitting atop his camel the revered Prophet Mohammed gave a "Farewell Sermon" from the Mount of Arafat during the 10th pilgrimage to Makka (10th year of the Islamic calendar). It was later also called the "Farewell Pilgrimage" as it was Mohammed's first and final pilgrimage to Makka before his death.

CITIES WITHIN
ARABIA

SAUDI ARABIA

JORDAN

IRAQ

IRAN

• TABUK

NEUTRAL ZONE

KUWAIT

ARABIAN GULF

HEJAZ

• YANBU

• MEDINA

JUBAIL QATIF
DAMMAM
DHAHRAN
KHOBAR

BAHRAIN
QATAR

DARIYAH •

• HOFUF

RED SEA

RIYADH

AL HASA

U.A.E.

JEDDAH •
MAKKAH •
• TAIF

NAJD

ASIR

THE EMPTY QUARTER

• ABHA

OMAN

YEMEN

P.D.R. OF YEMEN

ARABIAN SEA

DJIBOUTI

GULF OF ADEN

N

SOMALIA

| KM. | 200 | 400 | 600 |
| Mi. | 200 | 400 | 600 |

MAKKA

"IN THE KINGDOM OF SAUDI ARABIA ALL ROADS LEAD TO MAKKA."

Makka, one of the last forbidden cities in the world, is the birthplace of the Prophet Mohammed and the religious capital of the Islamic faith. This holiest of Islamic cities is impassable to non-Muslims, thus very few Westerners have the opportunity to go within the forbidden borders. There is a checkpoint along the Jeddah highway that must be passed before entering Makka and all non-Muslims must take a detour around the city. The Great Mosque, dating back to the 8th century, overflows with Muslims praying to their God, Allah. Al Haram, as it is called, is an impressive sight that remains with the visiting pilgrims forever. Twin minarets guard the entrance to the Great Mosque like soldiers doing their duty. Inside the mosque, which can hold 300,000 people, is the Holy Kaaba and the spring called Zam Zam. Outside the Great Mosque of Makka bazaars offer prayer carpets, prayer beads and finely printed Qurans for the pilgrims to take home as a memory of their hajj to Makka. Over a million pilgrims visit this beautiful mosque each year, providing Makka with its chief income. Makka is busiest during the month of Dhu al Hijjah, when the annual pilgrimage is performed, and is comparatively quiet during the off season.

Located in a valley between two hills, Makka, with a population today of over half a million, grew and prospered as a major Arabian trading center along the camel caravan route during the heyday of frankincense and myrrh. Long before the Prophet Mohammed and Islam it was know for its many sacrificial altars and sacred shrines, and also the yearly trade fairs at Ukaz, just outside of Makka. Mohammed conquered Makka in 630 AD with the aid of 10,000 followers and declared it the center of Islam. He denounced and destroyed all the pagan idols except the Kaaba. There followed a series of rulers in Makka after Mohammed — the caliphs, the Carmathi, Egyptian Mamelukes, the Turks, and finally its present day ruler, the Saud family.

DID YOU KNOW THAT . . .
During renovating construction of the Great Mosque in Makka, Western engineers had to perform their job outside the forbidden city of Makka with the help of remote television cameras.

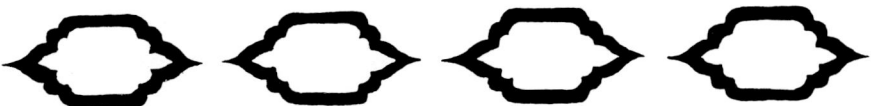

MEDINA

Medina is the second holiest city of Islam and is located in a flourishing oasis of date palms, fruit trees and fields of grain. Many pilgrims stopover in Medina en route to Makka to visit the numerous religious and historical sites. These sites include Mohammed's tomb, the very essence of the city, and his daughter Fatimah's tomb; the tomb of Aran; the Mosque of Quba (the first mosque in Islamic history); and finally the Prophet's Mosque. It was in Medina that the Prophet Mohammed's Islamic following grew after his flight from Makka. Yathrib was the city's name before Mohammed's arrival, but it soon become known as Madinat al Nabi — City of the Prophet, and is now simply known as Medina.

RIYADH

The capital and largest city in Saudi Arabia is located in a fertile valley within the high plateaus of the central region. Riyadh is in a lush oasis of date groves, orchards and grain fields and in fact the extended meaning of Riyadh is "gardens" or "groves." Like a floating leaf in a sea of sand

Riyadh is surrounded by desert and experiences much hotter summers than the coastal cities, and has colder winters.

From 1891 until 1902 the Rashids ruled Riyadh, having taken over from the Sauds. In 1902 the Sauds regained control from the rival Rashids, under the leadership of Abdul Aziz (Ibn Saud). Riyadh was proclaimed the capital of the Kingdom of Saudi Arabia in 1932.

To see Riyadh today makes it difficult to realize that only several decades ago Riyadh was a small town surrounded by walls built under the command of Abdul Aziz Ibn Saud to protect themselves from enemies. It took 40 days to build the encompassing walls that had only five gates facing various directions. Although at the time the western world was driving cars and resting in the comfort of their air-conditioned homes these were luxuries for only a few of Riyadh's residents.

JEDDAH

Jeddah located on the Red Sea coast, is one of the oldest cities in the world, and has been a crossroads for trade for thousands of years and handling the arrival of pilgrims on the last leg of a long journey to Makka for centuries. Jeddah offers you an international flavor with over a million people of all nationalities living in this cosmopolitan city. During 1985, Jeddah's diplomatic area changed as the foreign embassies moved to Riyadh, the capital.

AL KHOBAR

This eastern costal city was a small fishing village up until oil was discovered in the 1930's. Today al Khobar is a sprawling metropolis that blends unperceivingly into its neighboring cities, Dammam and Dhahran. Al Khobar is the center for business in the Eastern province, including for the time being the main international airport for that region. I say, for the time being, as a new airport is under construction in Safwa (approximately 30 minutes north of Dammam). Not far from the city center of al Khobar is located Half Moon Beach which is frequented by residents from all over the Eastern province and even many people from as far as Riyadh.

Al Khobar now joins to Bahrain with the help of a 20 mile bridge, complete with customs facilities in the center island, as well as two towering restaurants on either side of the border.

ABHA

Abha, the capital of the Asir region, is located in the heart of the fertile Asir mountains along the west. Not far from Abha is Saudi Arabia's first national park. Due to the high elevation Abha has a cool summer and an even colder winter. The mountain scenery here is breathtaking. Olive trees seem to go on forever, there are over 500 million. However they are not harvested, although olive production is in future plans.

DHAHRAN

Unfolding out of the barren sands and weather hewn hills, Dhahran has developed into a flourishing city since oil was discovered over 40 years ago. Dhahran is an important oil center, the heart of ARAMCO (the oil company formed by the original geologists who worked so hard to discover the oil fields of Arabia). The University of Petroleum and Minerals is located here. Dhahran comes from the Arab word 'dahar' meaning "back" (back of Dammam and Al Khobar) and also means high place. Dhahran is situated on a hill. ARAMCO created this city for its employees and their families, which includes within its fence schools, stores, recreation facilities and a golf course to name just a few.

HOFUF

Hofuf is located inland in the Eastern province in the largest inhabited spring-fed oasis in the world. This ancient city is located amidst a seemingly infinite sea of date palms. It is well worth a visit to Hofuf to see the souq al-khamees (Thursday market), camel and sheep markets, basket market, to explore the Jebel Qara caves and the pottery caves. Hofuf is the capital of the Al Hasa region.

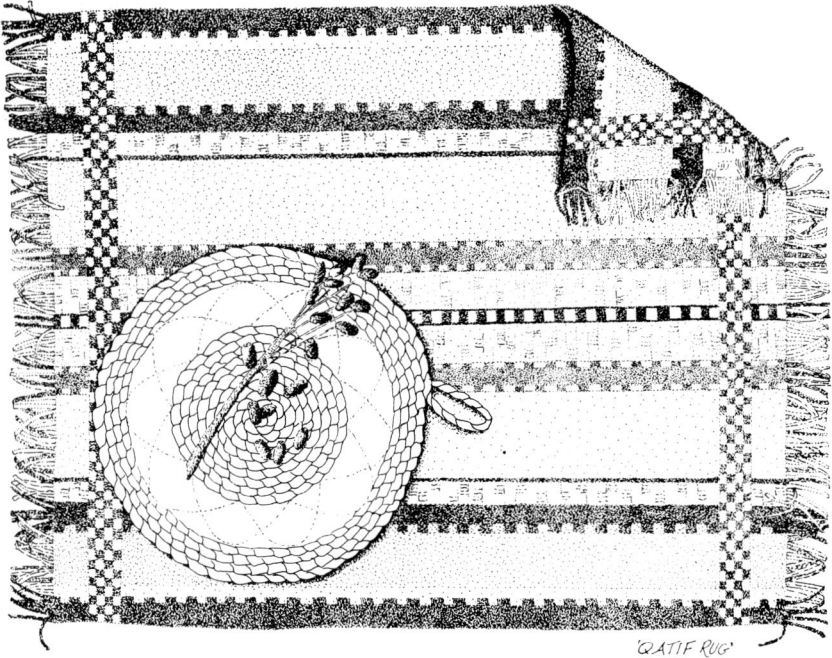
'QATIF RUG'

QATIF

The ancient oasis of Qatif, which lies on the coast of the Arabian Gulf
north of the tri-cities of Khobar, Dammam and Dhahrain, is an immense
area abounding in palm groves due to the ample supply of underground
sweet water. Across a short stretch of water from the gardens of Qatif is
Tarut Island which also has date palm groves. Tarut, one of the most
ancient cities in the Gulf area, has ruins to roam through on the island.
The markets of Qatif are a shoppers paradise for local crafts. Appropriately,
'Qatif' means "harvest."

DAMMAM

Dammam is an old and more conservative city especially compared to the
more modern adjoining cities of Dhahran and al Khobar. As the Kingdom's
major eastern port Dammam represents the capital of the Eastern province.
Only sixty years ago Dammam was barren desert settled by the Dowasir
tribe. They were given official permission from King Abdul Aziz to
return from Bahrain to settle in the area. There was only one spring for

water supply in Dammam. But Dammam soon grew when oil was discovered on the Dammam mound in 1938. As the oil gushed from the number seven well Arabs moved to Dammam for job opportunities.

THE JUBAIL STORY

Over an hours drive north on a super highway are the dual cities of Jubail, the old city and the new. A few minutes drive north of the old port city of Al Jubail on the Arabian Gulf lies the Industrial City of Jubail. Before the bulldozers and foreign workers arrived to build the new city, old Jubail was a small fishing and pearl diving village and was also famous for its slave market, abolished early this century. Today it is a bustling mixture of old and new crowded with foreigners looking to buy a bargain, while its sister city grows by leaps and bounds where once there was nothing but never ending sand.

In October of 1977 the Industrial City of Jubail was inaugurated,

"Al Tuwayah"

101

a city built from ground zero to utilize Saudi's greatest resources — its people and its oil. The project includes an 8 sq kilometer industrial area with fifteen primary industries, several secondary and a handful of support industries. Beside the industrial area, located along the shores of the deep blue waters, are large residential communities with health, educational, and recreational facilities that are all growing every day.

The site for Madinat al-Jubail al-Sinaiyah, the full Arabic name of this modern city, was chosen for several reasons — close access to raw materials, endless supply of sea water for industrial cooling purposes, deep water approach for a modern port complex, and finally, there was only sand at this site, so nothing was disturbed. In preparation for the industrial and residential sites earth was moved in to raise the level of the ground 3 meters, enough sand to fill 67,000 soccer fields one meter deep. In fact Jubail means 'hill,' named after the small hill that was located just north of the old city, itself removed and flattened. Landscaping and design of the city was all pre-planned, with suitable plants creating an impression of green blending into this desert site. There are well over a million trees planted, besides the immense quantity of shrubs and grass — Arizona palms, date palms, Australian gum trees, oleanders, 'camel' ivy, bouganvillaea, and well tended lawns.

Three canals for industrial cooling water have been constructed. One is for incoming sea water while another is for the outgoing water, which is said to be ecologically cleaner than when it entered. The center or third canal can be used for incoming or outgoing water when one canal is emptied so the accumulation of sand can be removed (blown in by the constant annual desert winds).

Jubail, found in The Guinness Book of Records, was the largest public works construction project in the world, congregating workers from over 60 different nations.

TAIF

This is the city that the Saudis go to annually during the piping-hot summer months. Taif, not far from Makka, is an ancient city situated high in the mountains above the Red Sea, 7000 feet above sea level and therefore enjoys a coolness throughout the year. Since the Royal family and Ministry personnel go to Taif during the hot months as well, to elude the scorching heat in Riyadh it is often called the "summer capital" of the Kingdom. Taif receives plenty of rain and consequently is an important agricultural area.

YANBU

Yanbu al Bahar means "fountain by the sea" and until recently was a restful fishing village. But now, just as in Jubail, but on a smaller scale, an industrial city has been built along the Red Sea in support of Saudi Arabia's petroleum production. Saudi Arabi's largest refineries are located here.

REGIONS OF ARABIA

There are five distinct topographical regions in Saudi Arabia, the Hejaz, Asir, Najd, Al Hasa and Rub al Khali — occupying nearly 900,000 square miles between the Red Sea and the Arabian Gulf (Persian Gulf to the Iranians). The Hejaz is a coastal region located on the western shores along the Red Sea and also includes the Hejaz mountains that rise to 9000 feet. Hejaz, which means "to isolate" or "to separate," is a holy region for the two holiest cities, Makka and Medina, are located here. As the mountains slope eastward they level out to a huge desert plateau. This is Najd, the arid heartland of Saudi Arabia where temperatures exceed 100 degrees F. daily. It is here that the bedouins concentrate, wandering among the drifting sand dunes during the winter and gathering in fertile areas such as Riyadh during the summer.

Southward, as you head toward Yemen, the Hejaz mountains rise more steeply from the coastal plain, reaching heights of 12,000 feet. This highly populated region is known as the Asir, which means "difficult" in Arabic, aptly describing the austere Asir mountains. The Kingdom's first national park was allocated in the Asir mountains where fields of juniper and sparse forests of green grow for as far as the eye can see and the views up the winding roads are breathtaking. The Asir region is largely cultivated as it has more rainfall than the rest of the country and even sees occasional snow during the winter on its usually blue-grey mountain tops.

On the eastern side of the Arabian peninsula is the large Al Hasa province, a lowland area rich in oil. This varied terrain of sand dunes, scattered oases, salt flats and gulf shores is named after the largest oasis in the region. Hofuf is the center of the date producing Al Hasa oases. Another large area containing many oases located north of Hofuf is Qatif along the Arabian Gulf. To the south, covering an area as large as the state of Texas is the Rub al Khali, or the Empty Quarter, appropriately called for its virtually lifeless terrain of shifting dunes. This largest single body of sand embodies the romantic and mystical images of the Kingdom of Saudi Arabia.

DID YOU KNOW THAT . . .

The Saudi flag is green with a white inscription and sword. The Arabic inscription reads "There is no God but Allah, Mohammed is the Prophet of Allah." The sword symbolizes justice and strength.

The national emblem of The Royal Kingdom of Saudi Arabia is a palm tree and two intersecting Arabian swords. The palm tree is a significant symbol of this desert Kingdom for from the bark to the fruit every part of the palm is utilized by the Saudi people. The swords, beside symbolizing justice and strength, represent the struggle it took to join the desert tribes into the unified Kingdom of Saudi Arabia.

The area of Saudi is about a quarter the size of the United States and the population of multinationals is verging on 10,000,000 and the government is a monarchy.

DID YOU KNOW THAT . . .

There are no rivers or permanent bodies of surface water in Saudi Arabia. You will find, however, a 'wadi' or dry river bed that overflows with water after rainfall, but soon dries up again. The oases of the desert depend on underground water. The water comes to the sandy surface forming springs or wells. The bigger the spring the larger the oasis. Some oases are made up of only a few palms, just enough for a weary traveller to rest by for the night.

GLOSSARY

abayah	black covering for Arab women
abu	father of
al hamdullillah	to God be thankful
Allah	the Arabic name for God
Aramco	Arabian American Oil Company
baharat	Arabic mixed spices
bedouin	Arab wanderer and dweller of the desert
bisht	outer cloak often worn by Arab men
bismallah	in the name of God
burghul	cracked wheat
burqa	a light-weight veil for women, with openings at the eyes
caliph	religious ruler, Muslim
cardamom	aromatic spice from the orient, popular for flavoring sweets, beverages, curries, and rice dishes
dellah	rotund bottomed coffee pot, slender neck and narrow spout
derwahza	Arabic door
dhow	a sea-going vessel
gahwa	coffee
ghutrah	triangular folded cloth worn as headdress
hadith	traditions relating to Mohammed, holds importance along with the Quran
hajj	pilgrimage to be completed on the 8th, 9th, and 10th days of Dhu al Hijjah, the 12th month of the Islamic year.
halat al-henna	night of henna
henna	powder dye used on hair, hands and feet; often a brownish red
hijra	migration (same word family as hajj)
hubble-bubble	water pipe for smoking tobacco
igal	part of the headdress, black doubled rope holding the ghutrah in place
imam	a non-cleric leader, in the mosque, studied in the Quran
Islam	a religion worshipping one God, Allah (stems from the 'submission to god')

105

jambiyya	crescent-shaped scabbard worn by the bedouins
Kaaba	block building in the Great Mosque of Makka, that which all Muslims face during prayer no matter where in the world they may be
kohl	a black powder used by Arab and Asian women to enhance the beauty of their eyes
Makka	birthplace of Mohammed, site of annual migration for Muslims from all over the world
mebkhara	incense burner
mishlah	similar to a bisht, outer cloak for men
miswak	stick from the Arak tree used for cleaning teeth
Mohammed	the prophet who spread the word of Allah
mosque	Muslim place of worship
Muslim	a believer of Islam
muezzin	the one who calls the Muslims to pray, trained in chanting skills
ouda	sandalwood
Quran	sacred book of Islam, collection of Mohammed's revelations from Allah
shamal	means north, also describes the seasonal windstorms of Arabia which generally come from that direction
Sharia'a	Islamic law
sheeshah	water-pipe for smoking tobacco
sura	chapter in the Quran
souq	market place
tagia	white skull cap worn under the ghutrah or on its own
taheeni	sesame oil paste
tamr	date
thobe	traditional dress of Arab men and boys, a floor-length shirt-like dress, often white
umrah	mini-pilgrimage done during any time of the year

INDEX

108